The Call to Righteousness

Bridges Youth Series

Kevin Stiffler,
Editor and Publisher

Carolyn Frost, Mary Jaracz, and
Virginia L. Wachenschwanz,
Layout and Design

Published quarterly for the teaching church by Warner Press, Inc., 1201 East Fifth Street, Anderson, Indiana 46012. Printed in the United States of America. For permissions and other editorial matters, contact: Coordinator of Publishing, PO Box 2420, Anderson, Indiana 46018-2420. Lessons based on International Sunday School lessons: the International Bible Lessons for Christian Teaching. Copyright © 1971 by Committee on Uniform Series. Scripture taken from the HOLY BIBLE, NEW INTERNATIONAL VERSION NIV®. Copyright © 1973, 1978, 1984 by International Bible Society. Used by permission of Zondervan Publishing House. All rights reserved.

ISBN-13: 978-1-59317-560-3

Warner Press

© Copyright by Warner Press, Inc.

Conte

MW00974320

About this Book

Getting the Whole Picture

Let's be honest: certain parts of the Bible are easier to read, easier to understand, more interesting, more directly applicable to life today—and therefore they are read, studied, and taught more. Have you ever determinedly embarked on an "I'm gonna read the whole Bible" plan by starting at Genesis 1:1 and proceeding one word, one verse, one chapter, one page, and one book at a time? You might have made it into Leviticus (or maybe Numbers, if you were really motivated). All those genealogies and laws tend to blur together. So do the words of the so-called "Minor Prophets"—guys such as Amos and Hosea, Micah and Zephaniah, Habakkuk and Zechariah and Malachi. And some of the "Major Prophets" tended to get wordy—consider Jeremiah, which has 52 chapters, and Isaiah, which has 66! But even if reading through the pages of the Bible sequentially is not the best way to go, it does not let us off the hook. God still expects us to be grounded in the whole Word. What would life be like if your family picked and chose when to love you, or if the authorities picked and chose which laws to enforce? The BRIDGES Youth Series will give you a foundation and an ongoing plan to make sure you give your students the *whole Word*. There is a video on the Digital BRIDGES CD to help you specifically as you prepare to teach on the prophets.

The Word of God speaks for itself. The Holy Spirit moves as God wills. But one of the ways God has designed the Word to speak and the Spirit to move is through *you*, the teacher. No pressure, though. Make sure that you're prayed up. Commit yourself to teach and love and disciple and encourage young people for the long-term. And make sure that you're *studied* up. Jump into this book with both feet, perhaps even with a "cannonball." The Old Testament prophets have plenty to say to the youth of today—if you will be the channel through which they can speak.

Do some digging and enjoy the meal!

Kevin Stiffler

Kevin Stiffler, Editor

Portable Sanctuary

The **Portable Sanctuary** is designed to be copied and distributed to students at the end of each week's session. This handout will continue the ideas from the session throughout the week with additional scripture references, stories, journaling, and prayer topics. This will give students an opportunity to establish some daily devotional time that builds on a consistent theme.

Encourage students to use the Portable Sanctuary, and lead them in this effort by using it yourself. Allow time at the beginning of each session to review last week's Portable Sanctuary and have some extra copies available for any students who were not present last week.

Digital BRIDGES is an interactive CD-ROM available for purchase to supplement this printed book.

From quarter to quarter Digital BRIDGES contains different things such as a video introduction to the book, teaching tips, videos, songs (that will also play with just a CD player), interactive games, projection sheets, color pictures and slide presentations, links to some great Websites, and all of the printed curriculum in PDF format for you to customize and print at your convenience. These features can be used in preparation for and during your time in the classroom to enhance the teaching and learning experience.

Whenever you see (DB) in the book, it indicates a place where Digital BRIDGES can be used.

Authors

The Call to Righteousness
Sharon Bernhardt lives in Penang, Malaysia, with her husband and three sons, where she serves as a schoolteacher. She has written frequently for BRIDGES and also Pathways to God.

Righteous Requirements
Randy Archer pastors the Lents-Gilbert Church of God in Portland, Oregon, where he lives with his wife Alisha, sons Cody and Ethan, and daughter Julia. Raised on the West Coast, a graduate of Azusa Pacific University, he enjoys the incredible roller coaster ride of journeying with Christ. Randy loves being with family, surfing, good music, and great coffee.

Responding in Righteousness
Dana Wilson Lemón served on staff at New Life Bible Fellowship in Dallas, Texas, for almost ten years before recently taking a position at Our Children's House in Dallas, where she works with the families of children in therapy programs. She loves to read and spend time with her teenage son, Jareth.

Bible Background was written by Merle D. Strege, professor of historical theology at Anderson University.

Hot Spots

Changing Taboos

There was a Clint Eastwood movie in the '70s where a doctor removed a brain during an autopsy. The scene was portrayed in shadow, leaving most of the detail to the imagination: you could see only the shadow of the doctor on the wall as he removed the top of the skull and took out the brain. At the time, this scene was considered shocking and unique. Today, television-watchers can see multiple episodes of crime shows most days of the week where brains, guts, and severed body parts are frequently shown—up close and in full color. No shadows, and nothing left to the imagination.

Graphic portrayals of disfigured people were long considered a taboo for television and movies, but not anymore. And even if this standard continued to exist, it would be almost impossible to enforce. Unedited cell phone pictures and videos are texted immediately after they are taken, or quickly posted on the Internet. The Internet itself has no taboos. Search engines have the capability to look specifically for pictures, videos, and music. Inappropriate content is often accessed unintentionally, when someone is looking for something totally unrelated, or it is e-mailed as SPAM. Filters and other controls might help, but they can do only so much.

In the book *Every Man's Battle* (Colorado Springs: WaterBrook Press, 2009), Stephen Arterburn and Fred Stoeker describe the technique of "bounce"—training a person to quickly divert his or her eyes away from sights or objects that lead to lust or other sins. This technique can be applied when watching television or using the Internet—not just to avoid sexual images, but to avoid *any* images that might not be beneficial for disciples of Christ to see.

UNIT ONE
INTRO

High Expectations

SESSION 1

A Call for Justice

SESSION 2

A Call for Faithfulness

SESSION 3

The Heart of Worship

SESSION 4

Come to the Waters

THE CALL TO RIGHTEOUSNESS

The calling to be a follower of Christ and a son or daughter of the one and only God is a high one. It is a call to live authentically in our relationship with God and with others. As believers we are called to live every day in a way that glorifies the Lord.

Session 1 of this unit explores God's call to live just lives that are void of hypocrisy. Session 2 considers how sin leads us away from a God who is always pursuing a relationship with us. Session 3 helps us see that our hearts must be cleansed and our attitudes right in order to truly worship the Lord. Session 4 discusses God's invitation for us to come into a relationship with him and be satisfied.

A sincere response to God's high calling brings deep and eternal blessings.

Unit 1 Special Prep

SESSION 1—WARM UP, Option 2 (More Prep), requires newspaper articles describing injustice in the world. HOME STRETCH, Option 1 (Younger Youth), calls for markers or crayons. Option 2 (Older Youth) requires handheld mirrors. FINISH LINE, Option 1 (Little Prep), calls for envelopes and knowledge of an unjust situation in your community. Option 2 (More Prep), requires an opportunity for students to participate in a service project.

SESSION 2—WARM UP, Option 2 (More Prep), calls for sets of dominoes; a large, flat surface; and video footage of domino competitions. STARTING LINE, Option 1 (Younger Youth), requires poster paper and markers or crayons. HOME STRETCH, Option 2 (Older Youth), calls for a sizeable area to take a solitary nature walk. FINISH LINE, Option 2 (More Prep), requires a neglected area in the community that is in need of cleanup.

SESSION 3—WARM UP, Option 2 (More Prep), calls for video footage of various worship services. STARTING LINE, Option 1 (Younger Youth), requires a paper labeled *Agree*, a paper labeled *Disagree*, and masking tape. HOME STRETCH, Option 1 (Younger Youth), calls for a worship leader from your church to visit the class. Option 2 (Older Youth) requires music, printed devotional materials, and/or creative supplies. FINISH LINE, Option 2 (More Prep), calls for an opportunity and arrangements to lead worship for your congregation.

SESSION 4—WARM UP, Option 2 (More Prep), requires a healthy snack, a sweet snack, a *FREE* sign, and a *$2.50 EACH* sign. STARTING LINE, Option 1 (Younger Youth), calls for card stock or fancy parchment and fine-tipped markers. HOME STRETCH, Option 1 (Younger Youth), requires butcher paper and markers. Option 2 (Older Youth) calls for personalized invitations, prepared prior to class; you can also bring soft music to play. For FINISH LINE, Option 1 (Little Prep), you can use a copy of the Chris Tomlin song "Enough." Option 2 (More Prep) requires an opportunity to raise funds or collect food for a local shelter or food pantry.

Leading into the Session

Warm Up

Option 1
LITTLE PREP
Participate in a role play.
Chalkboard or dry erase board

Option 2
MORE PREP
Discuss world events.
Reproducible 1, pens or pencils, newspaper articles describing injustice in the world

Starting Line

Option 1
YOUNGER YOUTH
Identify hypocrites.
Reproducible 2

Option 2
OLDER YOUTH
Discuss hypocrisy.
Chalkboard or dry erase board

Leading through the Session

Straight Away

Explore the Bible passages.
Bibles

The Turn

Consider the importance of living a consistent life.
Bibles, chalkboard or dry erase board

Leading beyond the Session

Home Stretch

Option 1
YOUNGER YOUTH
Reflect on personal character.
Paper, markers or crayons

Option 2
OLDER YOUTH
Reflect on character demonstrated through action.
Paper, pens or pencils, handheld mirrors

Finish Line

Option 1
LITTLE PREP
Take action against injustice.
Paper, pens or pencils, envelopes, knowledge of an unjust situation in your community

Option 2
MORE PREP
Participate in a justice activity.
Opportunity for a service project

Bible Passages
Amos 5:10–15, 21–24

Key Verse
But let justice roll on like a river, righteousness like a never-failing stream!
—Amos 5:24

Main Thought
God expects us to live just and authentic lives.

Bible Background

Prophecy in ancient Israel should be understood as a historical and theological phenomenon that emerged in a definitive way in the eighth century before Christ. Amos, Hosea, and Micah were the first of these eighth-century figures, and their messages helped to define the prophetic movement of which they were key parts. They were not the first people in the Old Testament to be named prophets—Moses, Samuel, Nathan, Elijah, and Elisha were also a part of this list. The Hebrew Bible (the Christian Old Testament) uses the term "former prophets" to distinguish the books of Samuel, for instance, from the "latter prophets"—Isaiah, Jeremiah, Ezekiel, and the so-called "minor prophets" whose sermons and oracles were included in one scroll called the "Book of the Twelve." However, many scholars think that the term *prophet* was retroactively applied to these earlier figures after Israel came to understand the nature of the prophetic word. First Samuel 9:9 lends support to this conclusion. It is a later parenthetical insertion that explains why Saul and his servant have called Samuel a seer and reads: "Formerly in Israel, if a man went to inquire of God, he would say, 'Come, let us go to the seer,' because the prophet of today used to be called a seer."

In the eighth century BC there arose a series of individuals to whom came the "word of the Lord." They were the prophets, called to proclaim a word to Israel. At that time God's people were divided into two kingdoms—Israel to the north and Judah to the south. Judah lacked the fertile agricultural land and commerce enjoyed by Israel, but Israel did not have the religious center of Jerusalem and the temple. Thus Israel had to create a substitute religious center at its capital, Samaria. It is not easy to create new religious traditions, and the shift away from the Jerusalem temple was one factor that opened the door to religious syncretism (the combining of different beliefs) in the northern kingdom. Wealth and prosperity also contributed to the moral corruption of Israel's society.

It was this latter condition to which the prophet Amos directed his preaching.

We know next to nothing of the biographies of many of the prophets, and Amos is no exception. It is not so much their life stories but the prophetic word they delivered that distinguishes them. We learn in 1:1 that Amos was a shepherd from the village of Tekoa. He was thus an outsider in two respects. First, a shepherd was a person without formal religious credentials. Amos was not part of the religious establishment, the priestly class toward which ancient Israelites looked for divine wisdom. Secondly, although Tekoa was a village in the southern kingdom of Judah, Amos delivered his messages in the northern kingdom. Amos the outsider preached a sharp message of warning and coming judgment to the well-heeled residents of Samaria. His warning singled out the manner in which the wealthy had used the commercial and economic system to exploit the poor. Amos cast his clear eye on Israelite society and saw a large gap between rich and poor wherein the needs of the latter were neglected. In one well-known image, Amos chastised the wealthy for lying on beds of ivory in idleness while the poor went hungry. Crucial to this message was the prophetic insight that linked justice and righteousness. Justice defined human relationships while righteousness defined the human relationship with God. The prophet's message was based on the understanding that the two are closely intertwined: without justice there can be no righteousness and without righteousness there can be no justice.

OPTION 1 (LITTLE PREP)

Participate in a role play.

Invite class members to divide into groups of two or three. Ask students to think about times when they have experienced unjust situations. Or, if they cannot think of personal experiences, ask them to consider injustices they have seen demonstrated in the world. Invite the groups to perform short role plays of the situations. As each group finishes performing, write a summary of the injustice on the board. After all the groups are through, discuss the following questions:

- **How do you feel when you experience injustice?**
- **What injustices in this world disturb you the most?**
- **Why do you think there is injustice in the world?**

Say, **Injustice happens in our world—and it touches each of our lives.**

Warm Up

Note:

If you sent the Portable Sanctuary home with students last week, take some time at the beginning of this session to review and discuss their experience.

OPTION 2 (MORE PREP)

Discuss world events.

Invite class members to divide into groups of three or four. Bring to class some fairly current newspaper articles describing injustice in the world. (*Note:* You may wish to look at Reproducible 1 to make sure these articles will work.) Distribute one newspaper article to each group. As the groups read their articles, invite them to complete "What in the World?" (Reproducible 1). When the groups are finished, encourage them to share their discoveries with the rest of the class. You can use the following questions in order to facilitate discussion:

- **What surprised you about the article you read?**
- **What did you learn that you did not know before?**
- **Did you have any good solutions to the issue described in your article?**
- **How do you think God feels about this situation?**

Say, **Injustice happens in our world—and it touches each of our lives.**

Starting Line

OPTION 1 (YOUNGER YOUTH)

Identify hypocrites.

Make a copy of "Examining the Characters" (Reproducible 2) and cut out the descriptions. Ask for four volunteers and give each a "Character Says" card.

Explain to the class that there are four different characters they will learn about. They will hear a description of each character followed by some words from that character; they should then determine whether or not this person "walks his or her talk." Does the description of his or her life match what he or she claims to believe?

Read the first character description and then let the first volunteer read the character's words. Discuss with the class whether this person's lifestyle matches his or her beliefs. Continue this same process for the other three volunteers. The correct responses are as follows:

1. Joel's words are consistent with the description of his life.
2. Vanessa's words are not consistent with the description of her life.
3. Nikki's words are consistent with the description of her life.
4. Pierre's words are not consistent with the description of his life.

Ask, **When someone does not live according to his or her beliefs, what is this called?** This is called *hypocrisy,* or being a *hypocrite.* Remind students that you have already talked a bit about injustice. Ask if they think that Christians ever cause injustice. Explain that Christians who claim to be righteous but who purposefully cause injustice are hypocrites.

When you are ready to move on, say, **Let's see what the Bible says about God's people and injustice.**

. . . .

OPTION 2 (OLDER YOUTH)

Discuss hypocrisy.

Invite students to think again about the injustices they examined in the WARM UP option. Ask, **Do you think that *Christians* are ever responsible for injustice in the world?** Write the word *hypocrisy* on the board and ask students to describe a person who is hypocritical. Invite them to share (without using names) experiences where they encountered hypocrisy in themselves or in others. How did those situations make them feel? Explain that Christians who claim to be righteous but who purposefully cause injustice are hypocrites.

When you are ready to move on, say, **Let's see what the Bible says about God's people and injustice.**

Explore the Bible passages.

Read together Amos 5:10–15 and 21–24. Discuss the following questions:

Straight Away

- **Why would anyone hate to hear the truth?** The truth is only painful or embarrassing to us when we have done something wrong. Point out that this talks about a court scene—and in court it's the guilty person who hates for the truth to come out.

- **What emotions does God seem to have in these verses?** The first passage contains some pretty serious accusations, but it also includes encouragement to do right, and the hope that God will have mercy. However, the tone changes in the second passage; God sounds disgusted, frustrated, and angry.

- **What types of actions is God disgusted by?** List these on the board as students respond. God is upset over people taking advantage of the poor, oppressing the righteous, taking bribes, depriving the poor of justice, and hating the truth.

- **Why do you think these things bother God so much?** This is an issue of power and injustice. These people were taking advantage of the poor and the helpless, cheating and abusing people who had no way to defend themselves. And the people who were doing this were *God's people!*

- **According to these verses, what "churchy things" were God's people doing?** They were worshiping God through religious feasts and gatherings, with offerings to God, and with music and songs.

- **How did God feel about their worship?** He hated it, despised it, could not stand it, would not listen to it or accept it. Emphasize to your students that just because a person sits in church and sings the songs does not mean that he or she is truly worshiping God—or that God is pleased with his or her actions.

- **Do you think there are any churches today that God looks at and says, "I hate your worship services! I can't stand them! I won't listen to them or accept them!"? Would God ever feel this way about *our* church?** Invite students to respond, without lapsing into gossip about any one particular church. God is merciful and loving, but this passage is very clear: when we do not live out our faith through right and just actions, our worship is not pleasing to God.

- **Why do you think the imagery of a river and an endless stream are used for justice and righteousness?** Perhaps because water is powerful, with the ability to surge over anything in its path, eroding, moving, or destroying it. God's desire is for righteousness to be unleashed as a mighty river, pouring over all things and driving out all injustice. Justice and righteousness portrayed as water may also signify a cleansing of the sinfulness that was (and is) present in the world.

Say, **God wants his justice and righteousness to flood over all the world.**

The Turn

Consider the importance of living a consistent life.

Ask students if they can recall any other places in the Bible where we read of religious people living contrary to their professed beliefs and oppressing others. Remind them that the Pharisees of Christ's time were often called to task by Christ because they were not truly living out their faith.

Read together Luke 11:37–42 and discuss the following questions:

- **Why was the Pharisee concerned?** Because Jesus did not perform the prescribed washing ritual before sitting down for the meal.
- **What point was Jesus making when he responded about the cup and the dish?** The Pharisees were concerned about outward issues and appearances, but their hearts were full of greed and wickedness. They needed to be concerned with giving to others instead of concentrating on making themselves more successful.
- **Jesus said the Pharisees followed some rules well—but where did they fall short?** They neglected showing justice and the love of God to others. Jesus advised them to continue to follow God's law, but to also live with genuine concern for others. Since they were community religious leaders, they should not be perpetrators of injustice.

Say, **True worship of God includes devotion given to him—and love and justice shown to others.**

Leading beyond the Session

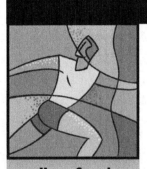

Home Stretch

Option 1 (Younger Youth)

Reflect on personal character.

Distribute paper and markers or crayons to students and invite them to spend a few moments thinking about their hearts and lives. Ask them to consider the following questions:

- **Is your walk with the Lord authentic?**
- **Do your daily actions truly reflect what you say you believe?**
- **Do you ever cause injustice, or have you viewed injustice in the world and refused to respond?**

After a time of reflection, ask students to create pictures that describe their lives on the basis of their answers to these questions. For example, someone might draw a person with two different faces if that person is struggling to live a life that is consistent with his or her beliefs. Encourage students to be creative in their responses. When all are finished, ask them to pair up and to share their pictures with one another. Encourage the pairs to spend some time praying for one another.

When you are ready to move on, say, **God expects us to live just and authentic lives—before him and before others.**

OPTION 2 (OLDER YOUTH)

Reflect on character demonstrated through action.

Distribute paper and pens or pencils to students. Provide several handheld mirrors for class members to pass around. (If there are enough for each student to have one, that is good, but not necessary.) Ask students to spend a few moments in silence, looking at themselves in the mirrors. Explain that even though a mirror is really for studying our external features, it can also help us think about our whole selves—including our inner features as well. Challenge students to use their time looking in the mirrors to consider who they really are, both inside and out. Present these questions for students to reflect upon silently as they look at their reflections:

- **Think about your inner and outer selves. Do they match?**
- **Are there some discrepancies between who you say you are and who you really are? If so, what are they?**
- **How can you be a person of authenticity?**

After a few minutes, provide an opportunity for students to share their thoughts. Do not pressure anyone to share, but encourage them to do so. Lead the group in a time of prayer, asking that God would help them to lead authentic lives that are free from hypocrisy.

When you are ready to move on, say, **God expects us to live just and authentic lives—before him and before others.**

OPTION 1 (LITTLE PREP)

Take action against injustice.

Prior to class, identify an unjust situation in your community. Perhaps there is an older or poorer neighborhood that seems to be neglected for street repairs or re-development, some poor residents who are being forced from their homes to make way for a shopping center, or a large corporation that seems to "skate by" when it comes to laws and environmental standards. Explain the situation to your students and invite them to write letters either calling for action from community leaders or encouraging the victims. Encourage politeness when calling for action. Action letters could be addressed to the local newspaper or to people who have the responsibility and the power to bring about a change. After students are finished, close the session by leading them in a prayer for the situation, asking God to help each of you to be just and to take a stand against injustice. You can address and mail the students' letters later in the week.

Finish Line

Note:

Don't forget to distribute copies of the Portable Sanctuary to students before they go.

OPTION 2 (MORE PREP)

Participate in a justice activity.

Prior to class, identify some ways that you and your students could work together to serve and reach out to those who experience injustice within your community. Perhaps your group could provide a children's activity time at a domestic violence shelter or serve a meal to the homeless. Involve your students in reaching out sincerely to those who tend to be neglected or overlooked by society. Say, **We have learned that God wants justice for the desperate and for those who cannot defend themselves. As we serve in this way, we are becoming the people God seeks—people of justice.** Close the session by leading students in a prayer for the people you will serve and asking God to help each of you to be committed to taking a stand against injustice.

Note:

Don't forget to distribute copies of the Portable Sanctuary to students before they go.

What in the World?

Your team has been given an assignment! You are a committee on justice and your task is to investigate a situation of injustice in the world. Read over the information given to you about the situation and then work as a group to answer the following questions:

1. What is the issue in this story? _____

_____

2. Who is experiencing injustice and why? _____

_____

3. Who is responsible for this injustice? _____

_____

4. How do you think you would feel if you were in this situation? _____

_____

5. How do you feel now as you read about this situation? _____

_____

6. How do you think this situation could be resolved or addressed? Devise an action plan about how to

implement your idea. _____

_____

_____

_____

_____

Examining the Characters

Description 1:
Joel loves football. In his opinion, it is the perfect sport. When he is not in class, he is either watching a game or playing in a game. When he is in class, he is most likely daydreaming about someday being drafted by a pro team. If Joel did not have football, he would have no goals or purpose in life. Football means everything to him.

Character Says 1:
"Did you see it? Did you see the Patriots stomp on the Seahawks? Kevin said he really needed my help at his mom's house, but I couldn't miss any part of that killer game. I know that Kevin would feel guilty later if he was responsible for my missing it. Church, you say? Or youth group? Naw, I don't see a need for them. No football there, and man, football is, like, the most important thing in my life. No need to bother with church."

Description 2:
Vanessa is really popular, and she makes friends easily. People describe her as "friendly, outgoing, and a nice person." Although Vanessa has never professed faith in any religion, she does not seem to have any bad habits or attitudes. There is not a single person who has a negative thing to say about her.

Character Says 2:
"I can't really say that I'm happy right now. Actually, I'm very depressed. I'm tired of living up to this 'goody-two-shoes' bit. It's not that I have some wild side to explore; I just get tired of not telling people what I really think and feel. For example, I'll never forgive Jeff for betraying my confidence. I hate him for it, and I'll hate him forever—but he'll probably never know. I can't stand Jessica this year, either. I wish she would just drop off the face of the earth! Now that would bring me great happiness."

Description 3:
Nikki can always be found in church on Sundays and Wednesdays. She is very involved in choir and youth group, and regularly helps out in the church nursery. She also enjoys volunteering for community ministry trips and is always finding ways to reach out and help others. Nikki's friends describe her as a good listener.

Character Says 3:
"I really do love to help others. I hope that it makes them feel good, but it makes me feel really good too. I'm definitely not perfect and I don't always say and do the things I should, but I give my best at whatever I do. I am encouraged because I know that God is still working on me."

Description 4:
Pierre goes to church and participates in most of the activities there. People at church are really impressed with the leadership that he demonstrates. Pierre hopes to find a way to help fund his college education. He plans to study at a Christian college and to pursue a degree in ministry. Pierre's congregation is really proud of him.

Character Says 4:
"I cheated on my assignment today. I didn't have time to do it because I was at Devon's party until 2:00 AM. I've cheated all semester, actually—but math doesn't mean much in the overall scheme of things. I know how to do it, so doing the assignments on my own is not really important. I know a lot of people who do worse stuff than I do. It's not like I'm doing drugs or sleeping around like some of the 'Christians' I know."

Portable Sanctuary

Day 1

Weak Witness

Kelli admits that it's difficult for her to consider converting to Christianity because of the Christians she has encountered. Many of them have told her that they know "the Way" and they claim to have found holiness, but they don't live any differently from non-Christians. In fact, sometimes they live even worse! Kelli also struggles with the way some Christians lack accountability for their actions, dismissing sin because "Christ forgives all." The greatest obstacle to Kelli embracing faith in Christ is the pride and hypocrisy of Christians. God knows our hearts and wants us to be honest and humble in our relationship with him and with others. That is what non-Christians want too.

Questions and Suggestions

• What is the state of your heart and your relationship with God? Are non-Christians encouraged to follow Christ or *discouraged* from following him when they interact with you?

• Journal about the ways your faith is visible in your life.

Day 2

Super Spirituality

Have you ever met a person who flaunted his or her spirituality as if it were a special talent? Oftentimes those who proclaim their own spirituality are really trying to hide some behavior that does not honor God. But those who *really* live for the Lord do so humbly, and the light of Christ shines through them as a result of their devotion to him.

The spirituality that others see in them is not fake and it's not just for show—it's a natural response to an open and intimate relationship with God.

Questions and Suggestions

- Read Matthew 6:5–6. What is the difference between a hypocrite in prayer and being a sincere believer in prayer?
- What type of response does this passage say Christ is calling for in your life? Pray about it.

Day 3
Our Just Lord

Psalm 11:7 says, "For the LORD is righteous, he loves justice; upright [people] will see his face." As a God who is holy, God can stand for only what is right and good. As people who seek to follow God, we too should embrace justice. Sometimes it seems like an uphill battle, and we feel that injustice and wickedness will win out. Maybe evil wins the battle sometimes—but it won't win the war. Regardless of the suffering we might experience in this life, God promises that just and upright people will see his face.

Questions and Suggestions

- Read all of Psalm 11. How can you embrace justice in your day-to-day life?
- Using a concordance, look up scriptures that talk about the justice of God. What does this tell you about God's character?

Day 4
Dilemma

As Aaron walked down the hall he saw that the "thugs" were at it again. Jared's bag and books lay scattered on the floor, his hair was messed up, and his eyeglasses hung precariously from one ear. "It's all I have, guys," Jared pleaded. "Please leave me alone. I can't give you anymore."

"You'll give us what we want, punk!" snarled one of the biggest kids. Aaron paused in the hall. Should he intervene? Jared sounded really desperate. But if Aaron *did* respond, what kind of retribution should he expect? Would it really be worth it?

Questions and Suggestions

- How do you think Aaron should respond? Why? How do you respond when you witness injustice?
- Say a prayer today for those who are unable to defend themselves against injustice.

Day 5
Appropriate Action

His clothes torn and his body bloody, he gasped for help—but no one answered his raspy plea. With blurred vision he saw a priestly robe and neatly-manicured feet draw near—and then move away, unheeding his cries. A painful spasm and a silent moment—and then he heard more footsteps in the distance. The shoes of a Levite appeared, once again moving away rapidly, seeking escape. How could he bear this any longer? Finally there were gentle, warm hands, cool water, and rest. Who was this angel of mercy? Surprise—it was a Samaritan.

Questions and Suggestions

- Have you ever experienced a situation where a "righteous" person seemed to turn a blind eye toward a glaring need? Have you ever turned away from meeting someone's need?
- Read Luke 10:25–37. How does this passage speak to you today? Ask God to help you love your neighbors as yourself.

Leading into the Session

Warm Up

Option 1 LITTLE PREP
Evaluate the consequences of poor decisions.
Reproducible 1, pens or pencils

Option 2 MORE PREP
Assess the impact of a tiny action.
Sets of dominoes; large, flat surface; video footage of domino competitions

Starting Line

Option 1 YOUNGER YOUTH
Create a story about the progression of sin.
Poster paper and markers or crayons

Option 2 OLDER YOUTH
Discuss the slippery slope.

Leading through the Session

Straight Away

Explore the Bible passages.
Bibles

The Turn

Explore the covenant of the Lord with his people.
Bibles

Leading beyond the Session

Home Stretch

Option 1 YOUNGER YOUTH
Design a road map or directions.
Paper, pens or pencils

Option 2 OLDER YOUTH
Participate in a "Stop and Turn" walk.
Sizeable area to take a solitary nature walk

Finish Line

Option 1 LITTLE PREP
Complete and discuss "The Change."
Bibles, Reproducible 2, pens or pencils

Option 2 MORE PREP
Make a positive change.
Neglected area in the community that is in need of cleanup

SESSION 2

A CALL FOR FAITHFULNESS

Bible Passages
Hosea 4:1–4; 7:1–2; 12:7–10; 14:1–4

Key Verse
There is no faithfulness, no love, no acknowledgement of God in the land.
—Hosea 4:1

Main Thought
Sin leads us away from a God who is always willing to accept us.

Bible Background

Like Amos, the prophet Hosea delivered his message to the people of the northern kingdom of Israel in the eighth century BC. There is reason to believe that the two men were contemporaries, for they were both active during the reign of Jeroboam son of Jehoash (cf. Amos 1:1, Hosea 1:1). It has already been stated that we know very little of the biographies of the prophets, and that is also true of Hosea—except for one major exception. The text tells us that he was directed by God to "take to yourself an adulterous wife and children of unfaithfulness" (1:2). Obedient to the word of the Lord, Hosea married a woman named Gomer who bore two children named *Lo-Ammi* and *Lo-Ruhamah*. These are symbolic names meaning "Not my people" and "Not pitied," respectively. Hosea's disastrous marriage mirrored Israel's broken covenant with God. The Ten Commandments expressly state that the people of God are to have no other gods before the Lord, but the people of the northern kingdom had violated this commandment, and the Book of Hosea likens such disobedience to the way adultery violates a marriage covenant.

The religious adultery of the northern kingdom of Israel took the form of religious syncretism, the blending of two or more different religious systems. The northern kingdom was politically separated from the south and its capital, Jerusalem. Jerusalem was the site of the temple, which made it the religious center of the nation as well as the political capital. When the kingdom divided after the reign of Solomon, the northern kingdom of Israel went its own way politically and religiously, severed from its moorings to the temple. The development of a new religious center made easier the possibility of blending the religion of the Lord God with elements of Baalism, the Canaanite fertility religion. The potential for the Israelites to slip into the worship of Baal had been a threat ever since the days of the judges. The northern kingdom's disconnection from the temple increased that threat, and by the time of Hosea the threat had become reality.

In God's eyes the religious syncretism (blending of religions) of the Israelites was a heinous sin. Idolatry breaks the covenant with the one true God. The texts for today's session extend the sin of Israel's broken covenant into the moral dimension of the people's lives. There was no faithfulness or love of God in the land—"only cursing, lying and murder, stealing and adultery" (4:2). Once again, as with Amos also, in Hosea we see the prophetic connection between righteousness and justice. Because Israel had lost their righteousness, because their relationship with the Lord God had been severed, they had also lost justice and slipped into moral chaos. To commit injustice is also to break faith with God, whose commandments require his people to treat their neighbors equitably. As Jesus said, the second commandment is like unto the first. Hosea used the language of the law courts to express God's position: "The LORD has a charge to bring against you who live in the land" (4:1), and "I remember all their wicked deeds" (7:2).

The people of the northern kingdom mistook their prosperity as a sign of God's blessing. They boasted of their wealth, taking it as confirmation that the Lord blesses the righteous and punishes the wicked. But wealth can also be ill-gotten, in which case the wrath of the Lord will break out against those who have neglected justice and righteousness.

OPTION 1 (LITTLE PREP)

Evaluate the consequences of poor decisions.

Warm Up

Ask students to think about times they have made a mistake by falling prey to some sort of temptation and to think about the results, or consequences, of the choices they made. Divide the class into groups of three or four students each. Distribute copies of "The Aftermath" (Reproducible 1) and ask the groups to work together to respond to the situations. After a few minutes, review the different situations and invite the groups to share their responses with the rest of the class.

Say, **Sometimes choices that seem to be small or insignificant can have a major impact on our lives.**

> *Note:*
>
> If you sent the Portable Sanctuary home with students last week, take some time at the beginning of this session to review and discuss their experience.

. . . .

OPTION 2 (MORE PREP)

Assess the impact of a tiny action.

Bring to class some sets of dominoes. Divide the class into groups to correspond to the number of domino sets you have. Challenge students to see which group can make the largest or most unique setup (in "chain reaction fashion") of dominoes before knocking it down. You could also have the whole class work together carefully as a team to create a design with their dominoes before starting it tumbling. If possible, show footage of a large-scale domino competition. Point out that with your groups (or on the video) there is often great distress when a portion of the setup is destroyed by a careless error. With professional teams the designs are often segmented in order to keep the entire structure from falling if a mistake occurs.

After students have demonstrated their setups, emphasize how amazing it is that one tiny action can cause such immense change. All the reactions of dominoes falling over within a huge design are started in motion by one little touch.

Say, **Many of the small choices we make in our lives today can have a major impact on our lives for years to come.**

> *Note:*
>
> There is footage of domino competitions available on the Digital BRIDGES CD; you can also find pertinent videos at www. youtube.com.

21

Starting Line

OPTION 1 (YOUNGER YOUTH)

Create a story about the progression of sin.

Divide the class into small groups (you can use the same groups from WARM UP) and distribute poster paper and markers or crayons to the groups. Ask the members of each group to pick a fictitious name of the person who will be their main character. Explain that you will give each group a statement about the main character and then the group should work together to complete a story about the character's journey to destruction. Groups should make picture stories (like a cartoon strip) describing the chain of events for their characters and illustrating a chain of continuous choices that do not honor God. Ask the groups to be realistic about the steps the characters might take. Here are some possible statements to give to the groups (you can give the same or different statements to each group or even make up some of your own reflecting a temptation that youth are facing today):

1. *(Character name)* **just cheated on his or her science exam.**
2. *(Character name)* **just told a secret he or she had promised to keep.**
3. *(Character name)* **just lied to his or her parents.**
4. *(Character name)* **just tried his or her first joint.**

After a few minutes, invite the groups to share their stories with the rest of the class. Ask, **Are these stories realistic?** Help your students to see that when we engage in sin it becomes easier for us to justify or rationalize other sinful behavior. Point out that the people of Israel had this kind of pattern in their lives. The sinfulness increased in each generation until eventually the people had almost no knowledge of God.

When you are ready to move on, say, **Let's talk about how the Israelites completely lost their connection with God.**

. . . .

OPTION 2 (OLDER YOUTH)

Discuss the slippery slope.

Ask students if they have ever heard of a "slippery slope" problem. Explain that a "slippery slope" is a situation where a course of action leads to another one, which leads to another, which leads to another, with unintended consequences in the end. Give the students an outlandish example of a slippery slope argument: **You should not eat bagels for breakfast. If you eat bagels for breakfast your stomachs will be bloated. If your stomachs are bloated, then you will not be able to concentrate at school and your grades will plummet. If you don't do well in school, then you will not be able to get jobs and the economy will come to a standstill as businesses go bankrupt.**

Invite students to share about times they have heard this type of reasoning used, and to create their own outlandish slippery slope situations.

Point out that in some situations there is validity to the slippery slope argument. Some people argue that the permission of same-sex marriage will lead to moral decay and the adoption of other behaviors such as polygamy and adult-child sexual relationships. Ask students to comment on whether or not they believe that reasoning is valid. Do they believe that society is becoming more sinful and permissive?

Explain that society has indeed become more liberal and permissive over time. Our style of dress has become more revealing, movies have become more violent and there is content that was not allowed before, behaviors that were not acceptable in the past are now permissible, and so forth. Yet as more is accepted by society, less is remembered about God and God's desire for our lives. This is the situation the Israelites were in during the time of a prophet named Hosea. They had moved far away from any knowledge of God.

When you are ready to move on, say, **Let's explore how the Israelites completely lost their connection with God.**

Straight Away

Leading through the Session

Explore the Bible passages.

Ask students how much they know about the prophet Hosea from the Old Testament. (Most of your students likely do not know much.) Explain that Hosea was a contemporary of the prophet Amos, both of them speaking to the northern kingdom of Israel (after King David the nation divided into two, with Israel in the north and Judah in the south) to make them aware of their sinfulness. As a way to vividly communicate God's message, God told Hosea to take an adulterous prostitute named Gomer as his wife. The relationship between Hosea and Gomer symbolized the relationship between God and his sinful people. Despite her betrayal, Hosea reconciled with his wife as God does with his people. Ask, **What do you think about God using someone's personal situation as an illustration? Why do you think God would use such extreme measures to reach the people?** Invite students to respond. The tangible way that God spoke through Hosea's life may have really touched the hearts of the people in a much deeper way than just hearing the preaching of a prophet.

Read together Hosea 4:1–4. Discuss the following questions:

- **What do you make of this situation in Israel? Could an entire country really have no one who was any good?** Invite students to respond. Perhaps there were no people left at all who followed the Lord. It is clear that things were bad and that the dominant behavior in the land was bad and getting worse.

- **This is the same nation that God miraculously freed from Egypt, led through the desert, and brought into the Promised Land. David—a man after God's own heart—had been their king. How could they have gotten so far away from God?** This deterioration was a process. The people began to fill their lives with other influences, crowding God out and going directly against God's will. God sent warnings through prophets such as Hosea, but no one listened. The people began to stray from God and their children also strayed; over time, the people moved completely away from God. If you have mostly "church kids" in your group, point out that the concept of worshiping and following God is completely foreign to friends whose parents do not know God.

- **What do you think it means to say the "land mourns"?** This is a poetic expression of the fact that the whole nation suffered. It also seems that the people's sin negatively impacted even the ecology of their land (animals, birds, and fish dying).

Now read together Hosea 7:1–2 and 12:7–10. Discuss the following questions:

- **What does this say about God forgiving ("healing") the people?** Whenever God got ready to help them, their sin would get in the way. Point out that God did not keep calling up the people's past sins—the people just kept on sinning! God's forgiveness was halted because the people did not want it; they had not had a change of heart.
- **What specific issue did God have with the Israelites here?** They cheated in business ("dishonest scales" in 12:7–10) and thought they could hide their wickedness behind their wealth.
- **Do you think this is still an issue in the church today? Explain.** Invite students to respond. Some businesses have the *ichthus* ("Christian fish" symbol) on their vehicles and business cards—and then come under criticism when their employees speed through traffic or rip off customers. Some feel that using the fish symbol is just a way for people to try to get more business, and that they should let their integrity speak for itself instead of trying to proclaim it with a symbol.

Now read together Hosea 14:1–4. Discuss the following questions:

- **In spite of their wicked behavior and the fact that the people had forsaken God, what did God invite them to do?** To return to God and seek his forgiveness, not counting on anything else to save them.
- **From this text, what can you gather about the feelings of God for his people?** God has unconditional love for us and deeply desires for us to be in relationship with him, even after all we've done. Point out again the fact that Hosea sought Gomer out even after she had been unfaithful to him. But just as Gomer was not forced to be reconciled to her husband, God does not force us into a relationship with him.

Say, **Like Hosea, God pursues a relationship with us—but God allows us to choose our response.**

The Turn

Explore the covenant of the Lord with his people.
Help your students to better understand God's covenant with his people by discussing the following questions:

- **If Hosea and Gomer were any other Israelite couple whose marriage vows were broken by infidelity, what would have probably happened? What about in today's society?** In Hosea's time, adultery was punishable by death. Gomer could have died for her sins. Today, they probably would have divorced.
- **How do these possible responses relate to our relationship with God?** Our sin is also punishable by death—and we are free to walk away from our relationship with God.

- **Read Micah 7:18–20. Why did God forgive the Israelites?** Because God loves to show mercy, and because of God's oath to their forefathers.
- **Read Exodus 32:13. What did God promise to the Israelites through their forefathers Abraham, Isaac, and Israel (Jacob)?** God promised to greatly increase their numbers and to give them a land to call their home. Point out that God becomes hurt and even angry when we forsake him—but God is faithful to his promises. Even though we turn away, God continually calls us to repent (turn back to him). God is God—he created us, and because of our sin and rebellion he could destroy us. But in his great love God continues to reach out.
- **What is God's oath or covenant with us today?** Read together Hebrews 9:15. Christ died to save and redeem us from the sin that would have resulted in our death. Explain that God still calls us to repent, just as he called for the people of Israel to repent. Remind your students of the gift of salvation promised to us through Christ's sacrifice. Encourage any students who have not accepted this gift of God to speak with you after class for further details.

Say, **God's covenant is to accept us, when we turn from our sin.**

Leading beyond the Session

OPTION 1 (YOUNGER YOUTH)

Design a road map or directions.

Say, **Is it always easy to return to God when we have strayed away? Explain.** Invite students to respond. Sometimes we are unsure of how to get back to God, or we feel that our problems are too great or that we need to "get things fixed up" first instead of coming to God for the help. Suggest to students that it might be helpful to have guidance or directions sometimes to find our way back to God. Distribute paper and pens or pencils and ask students to work together in pairs or small groups to design maps or sets of directions that detail how a person can return to God. Encourage class members to incorporate repentance, a sincere heart, God's generous and consistent offer, and other elements of today's study into their work. Provide an opportunity for the pairs or groups to share their creations.

When you are ready to move on, say, **God's Word and the Holy Spirit are available to guide us and to give us the directions we need.**

Home Stretch

Note:

If possible, display your students' work in your classroom or some other appropriate place.

OPTION 2 (OLDER YOUTH)

Participate in a "Stop and Turn" walk.

Choose a location where your students can take a quiet scenic walk—perhaps a park or wooded area near your church. Explain that you will all begin your walk from the same place, signifying the fact that birth is the beginning of life for each of us. As you begin to walk, each individual should choose a different path or direction, much as our individual life journeys are different. As they walk, invite students to think about their personal walks with God and to pray about anything in their lives that might need to be changed. Are there things they need to repent of?

Encourage students to immediately stop, pray, and then turn and walk in a new direction whenever they identify a need for change, signifying a change in the journey of their lives. Explain that they can repent of multiple things during their journeys. It is also possible that God may not bring anything to their minds as they walk; if this is the case, encourage them to allow this walk to be a serious time of reflection and prayer. Ask that students not seek out other students or socialize during the walk. Designate a common ending point for the walks, representing the common future with God that awaits those who follow him. After your walk is complete, solicit input from the students about their experience. If you wish, you can lead the group in the chorus of "Lord, Be Glorified" (selection 503 in *Worship the Lord: Hymnal of the Church of God*) or another appropriate song of worship.

When you are ready to move on, say, **God's Word and the Holy Spirit are available to guide us as we journey through life.**

Finish Line

Option 1 (Little Prep)
Complete and discuss "The Change."

Distribute copies of "The Change" (Reproducible 2) and pens or pencils and invite students to complete the puzzle and the questions at the bottom on their own or with a partner. (Bibles—preferably NIV—will be necessary.) Answers to Part 1 are as follows:

1. Consider (C)
2. Forgive (O)
3. Leave (V)
4. Temptation (E)
5. Repent (N)
6. Say (A)
7. Creation (N)
8. Christ (T)

The circles spell out *covenant*—a serious promise or agreement between two parties.

After a few minutes, bring everyone back together and discuss the questions on the handout. Close the session by leading students in a prayer seeking God's forgiveness and renewal in their lives.

Note:

Don't forget to distribute copies of the Portable Sanctuary to students before they go.

· ·

Option 2 (More Prep)
Make a positive change.

Identify an area in your community that is neglected and in need of care and ask permission from the owners to clean up the property. Explain that your group is looking at the concept of *repentance* or making a change in our lives and ask if the class can participate in making a positive change on their property. Ask your students to be polite and respectful and to work hard. Encourage them to seek other opportunities to help redeem people or to restore God's creation. Remind them to also resist temptation and to make choices that honor God. Close the session by leading students in a prayer seeking God's forgiveness and renewal in their lives.

The Aftermath

Situation 1

Bianca has always had a pretty open and honest relationship with her parents. They always talk about how she makes them very proud. She's never kept secrets from them in the past, but now she feels kind of awkward. Bianca's been dating a guy named Simon for the past few months. Her parents do not mind her being in a relationship as long as she puts God first. Over the past few weeks Simon has turned the pressure on and he keeps telling Bianca that she is the love of his life. Bianca has never been in a relationship like this before. She feels overwhelmed by her feelings for Simon. Simon's parents will be away for the weekend and he really wants Bianca to spend the night with him. She struggles with the decision for quite a while, but then decides to tell her parents that she will be at Cynthia's house. Cynthia will be fine with covering for her while she heads to Simon's....

What are some possible consequences to Bianca's decision to keep the truth from her parents? _____

_____

_____

Situation 2

Joel's friend Trey told him to check out the hot girls on a certain Website. Joel knows that he really shouldn't make it a habit, but wouldn't one time be okay? When his family heads to the store, Joel logs in to check it out. He can't believe what he sees....

What are some possible consequences of Joel's experimentation with pornography? _____

_____

_____

Situation 3

Tricia went clubbing with her friends on Saturday night. Even though they didn't discuss it beforehand, Tricia thought that she should probably be the designated driver. She was trying to have a good time, but it seemed as if all of her friends who were drinking were having way more fun. Tricia felt kind of left out. At one club this attractive guy started talking to her and bought her a drink. Suddenly her evening really improved....

What are some possible consequences of Tricia's decision to drink while out with her friends? _____

_____

_____

The Change

Part One

Complete the following puzzle:

1. Ⓞ ___ ___ ___ ___ ___ ___ ___ your ways and turn to God (Psalm 119:59).
2. ___ Ⓞ ___ ___ ___ ___ ___ one another (Ephesians 4:32).
3. ___ ___ ___ Ⓞ ___ your sinful ways behind as you experience life in Christ (1 John 3:6).
4. Don't give in to ___ Ⓞ ___ ___ ___ ___ ___ ___ ___ ___ (1 Corinthians 10:13).
5. When you ___ ___ ___ ___ Ⓞ ___, you are choosing to live in a new way (Acts 3:19).
6. Honor the Lord in all that you do and all that you ___ Ⓞ ___ (Ephesians 4:29).
7. When you give your life to Christ, you become a new ___ ___ ___ ___ ___ ___ ___ Ⓞ (2 Corinthians 5:17).
8. God sent Jesus ___ ___ ___ ___ ___ Ⓞ to redeem us because of God's great love for us (1 John 4:9–10).

What word is spelled out from the circles above? _____

What does this word mean to you? Write your own definition: _____
_____

Part Two

Respond to the following questions.

1. Have you done things that hurt the heart of God—even after you had already accepted Christ as your Savior?
_____

2. Was it difficult or easy to make the decision that did not honor Christ? Why? _____
_____

3. What was the result of your choice? How did it impact your relationship with God? _____
_____

4. Is it easy or difficult for you to repent? Have you already repented of all the things in your life that dishonor God—or are there more areas in your life that need changing? _____
_____

5. What have you learned through this session about God's feelings for you? _____
_____

Spend some moments praying alone or with a partner about the condition of your heart today.

Portable Sanctuary

Day 1

An Intense Relationship

God instructed Hosea to take Gomer, an adulterous woman, as his wife. This relationship was to signify God's relationship with Israel. The relationship was a powerful living demonstration for the Israelites of what God's love was really like. But have you ever thought about Hosea's and Gomer's feelings? What was this relationship like for them, particularly knowing God's purpose for their union? How did they feel about one another and their marriage? How do you think their marriage changed their lives?

Questions and Suggestions

• Read the entire Book of Hosea, paying attention to God's response to the Israelites' sinfulness.

• What speaks to you as you consider Hosea and Gomer's relationship? Thank God for his consistent faithfulness to you.

Day 2

I'm Not Worthy

A marriage should be built on love and trust. When love and trust aren't there, a marriage will often crumble. Gomer repeatedly betrayed Hosea's trust and she put aside the man who loved her to find affection in the arms of other men. Yet, whenever she returned Hosea would be there, loving her completely as he always had. Surely she thought more than once, "I am not worthy of this man or this love!" Don't we say that to God when we fall and God opens his arms wide? "I'm not worthy of your love, Lord!"

Questions and Suggestions

- Have you walked away from the love of God this week? Do you feel unworthy to approach God? How does it feel when you meditate on the fact that God still loves you?
- Read Romans 8:31–39. Journal about what God's love for you is like.

Day 3
He Can Relate

When you experience a difficult situation, who is the best person to give you advice? Isn't it often a person who has gone through a similar difficulty? That is the purpose behind support groups and online chat forums—people seek out someone they can relate to, someone who can really understand what they are going through. Christ understands our difficulty with temptation because he was tempted. Hebrews 2:18 says, "Because he himself suffered when he was tempted, he is able to help those who are being tempted." Not only did Christ suffer as we do, but he was victorious. This is added motivation for us to take our problems to him.

Questions and Suggestions

- Read the account of Jesus' temptation in Matthew 4:1–11. How did Christ respond to the devil? What does this tell you about the importance of God's Word?
- Pray that in the Word of God and the power of Christ you too will be victorious over temptation.

Day 4
Road of Repentance

Repentance is so much more than saying you are sorry. *Sorry* is simple, a quickly-spoken word that doesn't always indicate conviction or a change of heart. *Repentance* goes much deeper. Repentance requires action. When you make the choice to repent you are choosing to put the sin behind you and never pick it up again. When you repent you are making the decision to be a different person, to turn and go in a different direction. You will not live the same way anymore.

Questions and Suggestions

- Read Ezekiel 18:30–32. What actions are called for in this text? What are the results of those actions?
- Ask God to reveal any areas of your life that need to change. Repent and make the decision to change.

Day 5
The Wider World

Many times we act as if our own actions and choices have little effect on anyone else. Why would it matter to anyone else if I honor God in this choice? It doesn't affect anyone but me! In North America particularly we have bought into the lie of isolationism—sin is okay if it's committed privately, and it's not anyone else's business. We are very conscious of individual rights and as a result we often turn a blind eye to sin; we don't want to be offensive or seem judgmental. What will the consequences of this be? Will we reach the point of being a people without knowledge of God?

Questions and Suggestions

- Do you think that your individual choice to sin has any impact on your nation or the world? Why or why not?
- Say a prayer for your country and the world today. Pray that the knowledge of God will continue to increase.

Leading into the Session

Warm Up

Option 1 Discuss: What is worship?
LITTLE PREP *Reproducible 1, pens or pencils*
Option 2 View some times of worship.
MORE PREP *Chalkboard or dry erase board, video of worship services*

Starting Line

Option 1 Express opinions.
YOUNGER YOUTH *Paper labeled Agree, paper labeled Disagree, masking tape*
Option 2 Get a bigger view of worship.
OLDER YOUTH

Leading through the Session

Straight Away

Explore the Bible passage.
Bibles, chalkboard or dry erase board

The Turn

Discuss the need for purity in worship.
Bibles

Leading beyond the Session

Home Stretch

Option 1 Interview a worship leader.
YOUNGER YOUTH *Worship leader to visit the class*
Option 2 Participate in a time of worship.
OLDER YOUTH *Music, printed devotional materials, and/or creative supplies*

Finish Line

Option 1 Share the meaning of worship.
LITTLE PREP *Bibles, Reproducible 2, pens or pencils*
Option 2 Lead a worship service.
MORE PREP *Opportunity and arrangements to lead worship for your congregation*

SESSION 3

THE HEART OF WORSHIP

Bible Passage
Isaiah 1:10–20

Key Verse
Learn to do right!
Seek justice,
encourage the
oppressed.
—Isaiah 1:17

Main Thought
In order to worship
God, our hearts need
to be clean and our
actions should glorify
him.

31

Bible Background

The notion that the prophets of Israel were primarily concerned with the prediction of future events is often fueled by Isaiah's oracles concerning the Messiah. During Advent Christians read these familiar passages foretelling the Messiah's birth and the character of his rule. The prophets did sometimes predict future events, but more often than not their message concerned conditions of their own time. Prophecy, in a word, was as much if not more "forth-telling"—preaching—as it was *fore*telling. This fact applies to the Book of Isaiah.

Like Amos and Hosea, Isaiah also prophesied during the tumultuous events of the eighth-century BC. Unlike his two contemporaries, however, Isaiah lived in and delivered his message to the *southern* kingdom of Judah. Scholars date his life from about 742–689 BC. If these dates are accurate, Isaiah was a young man when Judah lived through a series of political crises. Israel, the nation to the north, made an alliance with Syria and waged war against Judah. Not long afterward the Assyrian Empire swallowed Israel whole and threatened Judah with the same fate. Anxiety and fear about Judah's fate preoccupied the minds of the political and religious leaders in Jerusalem. Isaiah may have been a member of this social class. From events mentioned in this book we infer that he had access to the king and the priestly leaders, suggesting that he was known to them in some capacity. Opinions vary about the specific nature of his place in Jerusalem society. Some believe Isaiah to have been a temple prophet, others that he was part of a circle of wisdom teachers and sages. What *is* certain is that he was deeply concerned about the moral and religious life of the people of Jerusalem and that he interpreted the political crises of the late eighth century BC in religious terms. Isaiah saw a connection between the calamities that threatened Jerusalem and its people's failed religious and moral life.

Isaiah 1—12 opens the book with a series of judgments against the city of Jerusalem. God's judgment would fall upon the city for its disobedience to the Torah. "Two features in this material are especially noteworthy. First, the harsh judgments announced by the prophet are roughly matched by promises that anticipate that after the judgment of [God] upon the city, there will be a renewal and restoration. That renewal and restoration does not in any way soften or diminish the judgment to come, but asserts that judgment is not the ultimate prophetic word to [God's] city."[1] The harshness of Isaiah's prophetic declaration appears in 1:10, where he addressed the Jerusalem leaders and people as "you rulers of Sodom" and "you people of Gomorrah," the infamous cities of the distant past destroyed by God for their great wickedness. Although modern readers often associate those two names with personal or sexual sin, Isaiah specified sins of social injustice. The imperatives "*seek* justice," "*defend* the cause of the fatherless," and "*plead* the case of the widow" strongly suggest that it was precisely such matters of social justice that Jerusalem had been ignoring at best and flouting at worst. That the city and its people had not sought justice made their worship nothing but a farce. Through the mouth of the prophet Isaiah, God declared that he has no interest in worship, no matter how fervent or proper, when the worshiper lacks a heart for justice. That Jerusalem was pursuing injustice had placed it in a precarious situation; divine judgment would fall. But restoration and renewal remained possibilities if the people would come and reason together with the Lord.

1. Walter Brueggemann, *An Introduction to the Old Testament: Canon and Christian Imagination* (Louisville: Westminster John Knox Press, 2003), 161.

Option 1 (Little Prep)

Discuss: What is worship?

Distribute copies of "What Is Worship?" (Reproducible 1) or show it as a projection. Ask students to complete the assignment alone, in pairs, or in small groups. After a few minutes, bring the class back together and invite students to share their responses. Some possible answers are as follows:

- Worship is defined as the act of showing respect, admiration, and devotion to someone or something.
- Examples of how people worship include with words, in song, in thought, in prayer, in dance or movement, in giving, in learning, and in posture.
- Requirements for worship include a person to do the worship, a person or object to which the worship is devoted, and a means or way in which the worship is expressed.
- Attitudes for worship include being willing to give something of yourself, being willing to receive or learn something, and being willing to focus time and attention on the person or thing being worshiped.
- Different places to worship include churches, synagogues, mosques, temples, in buildings, out in nature, alone, and with others.

Compare and contrast the different ideas that are expressed by your students, helping them to understand that not all worship is directed toward God, and that many different people worship many different things.

Say, **Not everyone necessarily thinks of worship in the same way.**

Warm Up

Note:

If you sent the Portable Sanctuary home with students last week, take some time at the beginning of this session to review and discuss their experience.

Option 2 (More Prep)

View some times of worship.

Show to your class some video clips from different worship services. Try to get a variety of styles (traditional, rock, liturgical, R & B, large choir, Catholic, Pentecostal, and so forth) and a variety of elements (congregational singing, responsive reading, prayer, special music, sermon, drama, choir number, and so forth). After watching the videos, ask students to identify the top three things they feel must be present in order for true worship to occur. Write responses on the board. Explain that not all worship is directed toward God, and that many different people worship many different things. All that basic worship requires is a person to do the worship, a person or object to which the worship is devoted, and a means or way in which the worship is expressed.

Say, **Not everyone necessarily thinks of worship in the same way.**

Note:

There is a collection of short video clips available to view on the Digital Bridges CD. You can also find a variety of clips at www.youtube.com.

Starting Line

OPTION 1 (YOUNGER YOUTH)

Express opinions.

Prior to class, post two signs, one saying *Agree* and one *Disagree,* on opposite walls of the room. Across the middle of the room, mark a dividing line on the floor using masking tape. Invite students to stand in the center of the room. Explain that you will read some statements and the students should respond to each statement by moving toward *Agree* or *Disagree.* They can also choose to stand in the center, which means *I don't know.* As you read through the following statements, stop periodically to solicit feedback, asking the students why they chose to stand where they did. You can also feel free to use statements of your own:

1. The best place to worship God is in church.
2. Worship is best when it is planned and directed.
3. Worship can include singing songs of praise.
4. Worship is a natural response of the human heart to God.
5. Attitude is important for worship.
6. People can worship God through their work (doing their everyday jobs or tasks).
7. Worship happens the same way for all people.
8. God is the only person I should worship.
9. Worship involves showing respect.
10. I enjoy times of worship.

Your goal is not to dictate right or wrong answers for these questions but to help students consider their own ideas and feelings about worship. Invite students to explain some of the ways that they most enjoy worshiping God.

When you are ready to move on, say, **Let's see what the Book of Isaiah has to say about God and worship.**

. . . .

OPTION 2 (OLDER YOUTH)

Get a bigger view of worship.

Explain that in today's society many people use the term *worship* to refer to a church service or, more specifically, the *singing* portion of a church service. However, Christians are not the only people who engage in the act of worship. Ask students if they can describe how people of other religions worship. Point out that Jewish worship services include prayer, blessings, and reading from the Old Testament, although they would not include preaching or choruses and hymns as we know them. Islamic worship services consist primarily of prayer, but they also include ritual washings, reading from the Koran, and sometimes even sermons. The biggest distinguishing characteristic of Christian worship today seems to be the focus on the singing of high-energy or emotional songs by the worshipers to express their love for God and gratitude for his blessings. In Judaism or Islam, the focus of worship is less on feelings or emotions and more on the religion's sacred written words and on fulfilling the requirements of the deity. Take some time to find out what your students know about the worship practices of other religions and whether they have family members or friends who belong to other religions.

When you are ready to move on, say, **Let's see what the Book of Isaiah has to say about God and worship.**

Explore the Bible passage.

Read together Isaiah 1:10–20. Discuss the following questions:

Straight Away

- **Whom is this writing addressed to?** Students will likely respond Sodom and Gomorrah, but direct them back to Isaiah 1:1. Isaiah was writing to the residents of Judah and Jerusalem. The reference to Sodom and Gomorrah is pointedly comparing the behavior of Judah and Jerusalem to that of the people mentioned in Genesis 13:13 and Genesis 18:20—19:29.

- **What was God's issue here with the people of Judah and Jerusalem?** They were "worshiping"—bringing sacrifices and offerings, burning incense, holding celebrations and feasts, praying, and participating in the feasts. However, God was burdened and tired of it, even saying that he detested and hated it, because the people continued to practice bloodshed and evil deeds, to do wrong, and to fail to help the oppressed, the orphans, and the widows.

- **Have you ever felt that God was not listening to your prayers or was far away from you? What was that experience like?** Invite students to respond. God promised never to leave us or forsake us (see Hebrews 13:5); however, this passage and others such as Matthew 5:23–24 make it clear that our hearts and our attitudes must be right with God before our worship is acceptable to God. The potential of God not listening should be fearful to any of us.

- **What does it mean to be oppressed? What do orphans and widows have in common?** Oppression is the cruel or unfair exercise of authority or power. Orphans and widows—in our society and particularly in the time of Isaiah—were at a disadvantage. God expects us to look out for those who are struggling and to care for those who don't have the power or the resources to care for themselves.

- **How would you contrast the positive and negative verbs used in this passage?** Invite students to identify the verbs as you write them on the board. The positive verbs might be identified as *wash, make clean, do right, seek justice, encourage, defend,* and *plead,* and the negative verbs identified as *trampling, cannot bear, hates, weary, not listen, doing wrong,* and *devoured.* The language indicating God's displeasure is very strong, and the words describing what God expects are very specific.

- **How did God's tone change in verse 18?** God actually said, "Let us reason together"! This sounds more like two people sitting down over coffee to discuss something than the God of the universe communicating his wishes to his children! God puts aside his anger and encourages us to think about our relationship with him. God wants to meet together with us and communicate with us—speaking to us *and* listening to us.

- **What does it mean to die by the sword?** To the people of the Old Testament, being secure in their own land was a clear sign of God's blessing.

35

If other countries came in and conquered you (this happened repeatedly—and the weapon of battle then was the sword), then it was a sure sign of God's displeasure. If we fail to follow God, then we can also expect to lose God's blessing.

- **After reading this passage, what do we need to do as individuals—and as a youth group or church—before we enter into worship?** We need to search our hearts and to live our lives caring for others as God desires—treating everyone with respect and helping the powerless and downtrodden in our society.

Say, **God expected the people of Judah to worship him with clean hearts and with actions that glorified him.**

The Turn

Discuss the need for purity in worship.

Invite a student to read Psalm 24:3–5. Discuss the following questions:

- **According to David, who can stand in God's presence?** The person who has "clean hands and a pure heart" and does not worship an idol or "swear by what is false." Help your students to understand the types of things that can become idols in our lives and the importance of truth in the life of a Christian.
- **According to David, what is given to this type of person?** The blessing of vindication from God. *Vindication* means to defend or to free from an accusation. Explain that just as our hands are cleaned by washing them, our hearts are cleaned or purified by confessing to God the things we have done wrong.

Now ask another student to read Matthew 5:8. Discuss the following questions:

- **How does this echo the promise of Psalm 24?** The pure in heart will see God.
- **What is Jesus' role in our having pure hearts?** It is through Jesus that we pray to God and it is through the sacrifice of Jesus that our hearts are cleansed.

Now invite another student to read 1 John 3:4–6. Discuss the following questions:

- **What is the effect of a person having a true encounter with Christ and placing his or her faith in him?** Such a person does not continue to sin.
- **Was John saying that real believers never make mistakes and fall into sin?** Point out to your students the presence of the word *continues*. A person without Christ can sin and not be bothered by it. If as Christians we should sin, then the Holy Spirit convicts us and we stop doing that sin.

Say, **Through the Holy Spirit, God purifies our hearts so that we become aware of the sin in our lives and turn from it.**

OPTION 1 (YOUNGER YOUTH)

Interview a worship leader.

Ask a worship leader from your congregation to visit the class. This might be your music pastor, the choir director, the song leader, the leader of the worship band, or even your pastor if he or she is the one who plans out most of the services. Discuss the following questions with your guest:

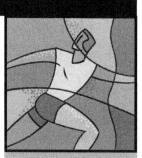

Home Stretch

- **How do you define *worship?***
- **How do you prepare to lead worship each week?**
- **What challenges do you face as a worship leader, particularly with respect to the expectations of the people in our congregation?**
- **How have you been affirmed by God and the Holy Spirit in your ministry?**

Invite your students to ask their own questions of your guest.

When you are ready to move on, say, **Each week our church seeks to offer worship that is pleasing to God.**

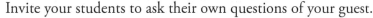

OPTION 2 (OLDER YOUTH)

Participate in a time of worship.

Make arrangements for your class to participate in a brief time of worship. Provide a variety of avenues for students to do this—perhaps some music that many of your students enjoy, some printed materials for meditation, some art supplies, and anything else that students could use to offer their worship to God. Say, **In light of what we have just learned, let's seek to worship God with clean hands and pure hearts.** Begin your worship time with some moments of quiet mediation, encouraging students to think about the condition of their hearts. Can they worship God in spirit and in truth? Is there anything blocking their relationship with God? Will God accept the offering and praise that they bring? If you wish, you can conclude this worship time by singing together something that is pertinent to the topic.

When you are ready to move on, say, **Each time we worship, God wants us to come with our hearts prepared.**

Finish Line

Note:

Don't forget to distribute copies of the Portable Sanctuary to students before they go.

OPTION 1 (LITTLE PREP)
Share the meaning of worship.

Divide students into pairs or small groups, distribute copies of "Worship with Us" (Reproducible 2), and ask the groups to work together to complete the handout. Explain that this work will be shared with the congregation, so it should reflect what you have been discussing today about purity of heart in worship. After a few minutes, invite groups to share their responses with the rest of the class. You can share your work with the congregation in one of the following ways:

- Work together to choose the responses that best summarize the opinions and feelings of the whole class; write these on a blank copy of the reproducible and have it included with the worship bulletins on a future Sunday.
- Post all copies of your students' work in a location where they can be read by the congregation.
- Make arrangements to have some of your students read their thoughts during a future worship service.

Close the session in prayer, asking God to search your hearts each time you prepare to worship him.

• •

OPTION 2 (MORE PREP)
Lead a worship service.

Make arrangements with your congregation's worship leader for your group to help plan and lead a worship service of your congregation. Your group's role should depend on the gifts your students have and the structure of your congregation's worship services. If you have musicians or singers in the group, they might play or sing for the congregational singing or provide special music or the offertory; other students might offer prayer during the service, do the announcements, greet worshipers, take the offering, and present a drama or skit. Your goal is to involve each student in a way that uses that student's gifts and glorifies God. As you plan for this service, encourage students to consider what you have learned about being prepared for worship, and to think about how they can help the congregation to also be ready to worship. You may consider involving your students in worship leadership on a regular basis.

Close the session in prayer, asking God to use you as you serve as worship leaders in your church.

What Is Worship?

Examples of how people worship:

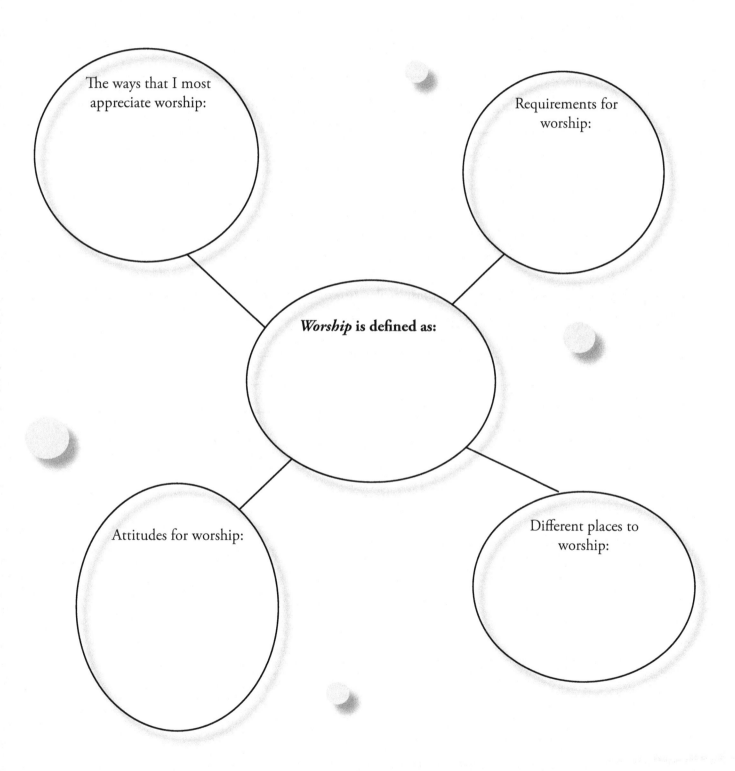

The ways that I most appreciate worship:

Requirements for worship:

Worship **is defined as:**

Attitudes for worship:

Different places to worship:

Worship with Us

Based on what you have learned about worship today, complete the following acrostic with statements that describe what worship really is and what God asks of us in preparation to worship him:

W_____

O_____

R_____

S_____

H_____

I_____

P_____

Using your Bibles, choose some verses that inspire you to worship God more completely. Choose three to five verses that you can share with others to encourage them as they worship God:

_____

_____

_____

_____

_____

Portable Sanctuary

NOTES

Day 1
The Heart of Worship

Megan was still fuming. Sitting in her usual pew, dressed in one of her usual Sunday outfits, and chewing on a wisp of her hair, she brooded. Her sister was being such a conceited brat—and her mom had the nerve to ground *Megan?!* "It was not even my fault!" Megan stewed. The pastor prayed, the music began playing, and everyone in the congregation stood and began to sing, but Megan just couldn't focus her heart on the Lord at a time like this....

Questions and Suggestions

- Have you ever felt like Megan? Has your heart been ill-prepared to participate in worship at church? What advice would you have for Megan?
- Read Hebrews 12:2. Pray that God would encourage your heart as you fix your eyes on Jesus.

Day 2
Fruitful Praise

Hebrews 13:15 says, "Through Jesus, therefore, let us continually offer to God a sacrifice of praise—the fruit of lips that confess his name." When we know God and have experienced the salvation afforded us through Christ, our natural response is praise—it grows and blossoms in our lives. The praise of God is natural for us—a fruit, a by-product of living in faith and knowledge of Christ. Our praise is a gift to God—a sacrifice that rises before his throne.

- Do you see the fruit of praise coming out of your relationship with Christ?
- Use a concordance to find other references to "fruit" in the New Testament and read those passages. Pray that spiritual fruit will be abundant in all areas of your life.

Day 3
The Wonder

Creation itself inspires awe and admiration in us—the raging rapids approaching a waterfall, the buzz of cicada wings, the growl of a hungry lion. The miracle of birth and the complexity of the human body also inspire wonder. What incredible things God has created! Is it any wonder that people have worshiped nature? Is it any wonder that human beings have sought to discover the origin of this amazing planet? The Creator of this universe deserves our worship and our praise!

Questions and Suggestions

- Read Colossians 1:16. All things were created by Christ—but what does it mean that they were created *for* him?
- Spend some time today worshiping God and praising him for his creation.

Day 4
Bowing Down

In Thailand the traditional greeting is not shaking hands—it is something called a *wai*. The palms of the hands are placed together in front of the body and the person slightly bows the head. The placement of the hands denotes respect. If the person is greeting a stranger, the hands will be at chest level. If the person is greeting an older or important person who is worthy of respect, the tips of the fingers will be on the chin. If a person is greeting a priest or other much-respected person, the tips of the fingers will be at the forehead. However, if a person happens to be greeting the king, the hands will be at the forehead and the person will be kneeling on the floor with the forehead to the ground. The king, the supreme ruler, is greeted with utmost respect. As Christians, how should we approach *our* King?

Questions and Suggestions

- How would you show respect to the president or prime minister of your country? Do you think people usually show respect to those in authority over them?
- Read Psalm 95:6. Take a few moments to kneel before God in prayer and worship.

Day 5
The Anointing

"What? Jesus is here? I must see him! But I'm so sinful, so dirty—I don't even have the right to approach him. What can I say? I am nothing—he is everything." Her mind raced and she felt such anguish and shame crushing her from the weight of her sins. Meeting Jesus was nothing like she imaged. She couldn't even speak. No words came. He was looking right into her heart. It made her cry and she wiped his feet with perfume, her tears, her hair—her heart. "I'm only worthy to touch his feet—nothing more," she thought. Then words pierced her very soul, filling her with tender warmth: "Your sins are forgiven."

Questions and Suggestions

- Read Luke 7:36-50. What do you learn from this moment of worship? How did the woman worship? What can you deduce about the condition of her heart?
- Has God been saying anything to you in your devotional times this week? What is God saying? How should you respond?

Leading into the Session

Warm Up

Option 1
LITTLE PREP
Assess two different invitations.
Reproducible 1, pens or pencils

Option 2
MORE PREP
Compare paying for something and receiving something free.
A healthy snack, a sweet snack, a FREE sign, and a $2.50 EACH sign

Starting Line

Option 1
YOUNGER YOUTH
Create an invitation.
Card stock paper or fancy parchment, fine-tipped markers

Option 2
OLDER YOUTH
Discuss "Too good to be true."

Leading through the Session

Straight Away

Explore the Bible passage.
Bibles

The Turn

Participate in a role play.
Bibles

Leading beyond the Session

Home Stretch

Option 1
YOUNGER YOUTH
Respond to God's invitation.
Butcher paper, markers

Option 2
OLDER YOUTH
Receive God's invitation.
Personalized invitations, prepared prior to class; soft music (optional)

Finish Line

Option 1
LITTLE PREP
Think about being satisfied in God.
Reproducible 2, pens or pencils; copy of the Chris Tomlin song "Enough" (optional)

Option 2
MORE PREP
Participate in a provision activity.
Opportunity to raise funds or collect food for a local shelter or food pantry

SESSION 4

COME TO THE WATERS

Bible Passage
Isaiah 55

Key Verse
Seek the LORD while he may be found; call on him while he is near.
—Isaiah 55:6

Main Thought
God invites us to find our provision in him.

43

The entire Book of Isaiah contains a dual message of judgment on one hand but hope on the other. Chapters 1—39 speak words of hope along with judgment, with judgment as the dominant theme. Beginning with chapter 40 the emphasis is reversed, with hope and comfort being emphasized over judgment. Isaiah 55 clearly illustrates this reversal and the dominant message of hope.

The people of Israel to whom Isaiah 55 was addressed were in desperate need of a divine word of comfort and consolation. Isaiah 1—39 addressed Jerusalem and Judah as a people who lived under threat, whether in the form of the alliance between Israel and Syria, the Assyrian Empire, or the Babylonian Empire. The eighth and seventh centuries before Christ were a time of political realignment in the region surrounding Israel and Judah. During the reigns of Saul, David, Solomon, and the early kings of the divided monarchy, the little kingdoms of the Near East prospered as independent states because the three great superpowers that usually dominated the region each suffered from political disunity and relative weakness so that they could not contest the other powers for dominance in the region. While the Egyptian, Assyrian, and Babylonian empires all slept through a kind of political hibernation, so to speak, the small kingdoms at the western end of the Fertile Crescent were able to assert themselves. In the eighth century that began to change as first the Assyrians and then the Babylonians reestablished control of the region. It was the Assyrians who utterly obliterated the northern kingdom of Israel in 722 BC and threatened Judah before giving way to the Babylonians; once in control, the Babylonians invaded and destroyed Jerusalem and its temple in 587 BC and in a series of deportations carried off a large segment of the population into an exile that lasted until 539 BC. The prophets who lived and preached during these tumultuous centuries understood these dramatic events *theologically*—they were not simply the rise and fall of great powers but the result of the hand of God. A prophet such as Amos saw God at work judging *all* nations, not only Israel and Judah. Nevertheless, it was specifically their failure to live in obedience to the word and will of God that was the focal point of the prophets' preaching.

In view of this broad history of the region it becomes clear that Isaiah 40 and following was addressed to people whose hope and confidence in God had been dashed by exile. Imagine the confusion in Jerusalem as Babylonian soldiers killed, raped, and plundered their way through the city before pulling down Solomon's temple, the house of the Lord. As they were marched across the miles into exile, the survivors of this ancient holocaust asked themselves such questions as, "Where is God?" "Why would God do this to us?" and "What will become of us?" The words of Isaiah 55 would have nurtured the flickering flame of hope into life once again by revealing that God was eager for the restoration of his people. These verses held promise of a new beginning and new relationship between the nearly hopeless exiles and their Lord. The new thing that God was about to do would be marked by generosity towards his people. Judgment was heavy indeed—so severe as to nearly break the people and destroy all hope—but it was countered by the promise of a restoration of such generosity as to overcome the pain that Israel had endured.

OPTION 1 (LITTLE PREP)

Assess two different invitations.

Distribute to students copies of "The Invitation" (Reproducible 1), or show it as a projection. Ask students to work alone or in pairs or groups to compare and evaluate the two invitations shown. After a few minutes, bring the class back together and discuss responses. Point out that Melissa's party offers lots of different activities, is "come-and-go" (no time limit), is free, and includes food, drink, and transportation to the event. Miranda's party requires guests to purchase their own tickets, includes only cake and punch, and explicitly states what sorts of gifts are expected. Some students may feel that a party is more about honoring the person who invited you, but Melissa's party does seem to offer more for those who are invited.

Say, **Most of us enjoy being invited to a good party.**

Warm Up

> *Note:*
> If you sent the Portable Sanctuary home with students last week, take some time at the beginning of this session to review and discuss their experience.

OPTION 2 (MORE PREP)

Compare paying for something and receiving something free.

Bring to class two different kinds of snacks, one type might be something healthy such as granola bars or fruit and the other something sweet such as donuts or cookies. Set out the snacks, placing a sign that reads *FREE* by the healthy snacks and one that says *$2.50 EACH* by the sweet snacks. Invite students to consider having some of the snacks you have provided. Do not comment on why there is a cost for the sweet snacks, but insist that the students pay if they wish to have the sweet snacks.

After students have chosen (or not chosen) their snacks, invite them to discuss the options. Compare the number of students who paid to the number who chose the free snack; then compare the number of students who would have *preferred* the sweet snack more than the healthy snack. Ask students why they chose the snacks they chose. Was anyone put off by the cost? Were students more prone to choose whatever was offered for free?

Say, **Most of us enjoy getting something for free—especially when it is something we really want.**

> *Note:*
> You can return students' money when this activity is through, or save it for the youth workers' retirement fund.

45

Starting Line

OPTION 1 (YOUNGER YOUTH)

Create an invitation.

Divide the class into groups of three or four students each. Give each group some card stock or fancy parchment and some fine-tipped markers and ask the groups to design invitations inviting people to join the family of God by accepting Christ. Encourage groups to be creative and engaging in their designs. Remind students that God wants all people everywhere to be in relationship with him, and that Christ came to make that relationship possible. In designing their invitations, groups should consider effective ways to interest people in Christ. When the groups are finished, review their work and display it somewhere in your meeting space.

When you are ready to move on, say, **Let's take a look at the invitation given by God in Isaiah.**

· ·

OPTION 2 (OLDER YOUTH)

Discuss "Too good to be true."

Ask, **Have you ever heard the statement, "If it sounds too good to be true, then it probably is"?** Invite students to brainstorm about times in their lives when that concept has applied. For example, maybe a student was promised a high-paying after-school sales job that turned out to be lousy, or maybe someone set a student up with a "dream date" that turned out to be a disaster. Say, **For some people, "too good to be true" is the story of their lives. What adjectives could you use to describe a person who believes this—who has been let down time and time again?** People who have been "burned" a lot do not have much hope in the possibility of experiencing anything good. Their outlook is negative and suspicious. These people suspect that others are not being truthful.

Now ask, **Have you ever experienced something that you thought at first was "too good to be true" but it ended up being true after all? What was that experience like?** Invite students to share about unexpected and amazingly good experiences they have had.

When you are ready to move on, say, **Let's take a look at something "too good to be true" that God offers us.**

Explore the Bible passage.

Read together Isaiah 55:1–7. Discuss the following questions:

Straight Away

- **What "beverages" did God offer here? What is the significance of this combination?** God offered the people water, wine, and milk. This may seem like a strange list to your students, but explain that this represented the full range of beverages that were available to the people of that time, from basic to fancy—refreshing and cleansing water, nourishing milk, and invigorating wine. Ask your students if they have ever been to a restaurant with one of the soda machines that offers dozens of choices. This was an offer of abundance—God would supply all they needed, and more.

- **What is required to partake of this offer from God? What is *not* needed?** God invites all who are thirsty to come, and money is not required—the offer is absolutely free.

- **How do you see people today trying to find fulfillment in things that do not really satisfy?** Invite students to respond.

- **What effect will we have in the world when we eat and drink from God's good offerings?** We will be witnesses to the rest of the world; people we don't even know will see that God is working in us and will also want what God has to offer.

- **Will there ever be a time when God cannot be found, or when he is not near? Is this idea consistent with what you have been taught?** Invite students to respond. As long as we draw breath on this earth we can choose to turn to God—but each of our lives here will end someday. In effect, there is a time limit on finding God. This is a very sobering fact—although God is always there, seeking to draw us to himself, there will come a time when it is too late to enter into a relationship with God.

Now read together Isaiah 55:8–13. Discuss the following questions:

- **What do you think verse 8 means?** Since God is omniscient (all-knowing), we will never be able to fully understand his plans and his ways. Not only do we not know all that God knows, we would not understand it even if it were presented to us. Even the things we do know about God and all the scientific knowledge we have put together barely scratch the surface of who God is, what God knows, and how God operates. Point out that this should be encouraging and comforting to us—we don't have to worry in any situation, even when we don't understand it all, because God is on top of it.

- **How is God's word like the rain and the snow?** The rain and the snow don't fall just to evaporate again—they water the plants and make life possible. God does not give his word just to hear himself speak—his words have power and purpose, and they always bring about their purpose. Again, there should be great encouragement and comfort in this—if God said it, we can count on it!

- **According to the conclusion of this chapter, what is the purpose of God's word in our lives?** It is for us to have joy and peace, finding it in even the mountains and the trees of nature around us. When we enjoy this joy and peace in our lives, God's name will be renowned (praised and honored).

Say, **Isaiah invited the people to seek God *first* for their needs.**

The Turn

Participate in a role play.

Invite students to look at Matthew 22:1–14. Ask for volunteers to assume the roles mentioned in the text and to dramatize the parable in this passage as it is read. Students who do not wish to act in the role play can participate by helping to narrate the passage as the volunteers act it out. After the story has been presented, discuss the following questions:

- **How did the first invited guests respond to the invitation?** Some simply refused to come, some ignored the invitation and went to do other things, and some mistreated and even killed the king's messengers.
- **How did the king feel about this?** He was enraged and punished the abusers.
- **Why did the people refuse the king's invitation?** They were preoccupied with their own lives and their own interests—their farms, their businesses, and so forth.
- **Why do people today refuse Christ's invitation for eternal life?** People give exactly the same excuses—other things are more important, so they ignore or turn down Christ's invitation.
- **Whom did the king decide to invite next?** He invited anyone who would come—good or bad. The messengers went out into the streets and brought everyone they could find.
- **What does this have to do with Christ's invitation to eternal life?** Jesus does not limit his invitation to some—it is open to all who are willing, regardless of who they are.
- **What happened to the man who was in the banquet without the proper clothes?** He was thrown out of the banquet and banished from the presence of the king.
- **Doesn't this seem a little harsh? What does this have to do with the invitation of Christ?** In order to be in the presence of God, we must be prepared. We need to accept God's invitation *and* be dressed in robes of righteousness (Isaiah 61:10), allowing God to cleanse us from sin. Explain that at an ancient wedding feast, the king provided the clothes for the guests to wear, just as God clothes us in righteousness.

Say, **This is an invitation from God, not a demand. The choice is up to you.**

OPTION 1 (YOUNGER YOUTH)

Respond to God's invitation.

Post on the wall a large piece of butcher paper with the words *In response to God's invitation, I am called to....* Distribute markers and ask students to think about the session and the verses you have studied and to consider what specific actions God is calling them to. Allow time for students to think and to write their responses on the paper. Ask those who are willing to share how they feel about God's challenge to them. Will it be difficult? Why or why not? Discuss ways that you can support one another in these decisions.

When you are ready to move on, say, **If God is asking you to do something, he will make a way for it to happen.**

Home Stretch

• •

OPTION 2 (OLDER YOUTH)

Receive God's invitation.

Prior to class, design and fill out a personalized invitation for each student. Prepare a few extra for visitors and write their names on these during the session. Each invitation should include the student's name and an invitation to come to God based on the Isaiah passage; you can also address current situations or challenges in the students' lives. For example:

> *Eric,*
>
> *You're invited to satisfaction and fulfillment*
> *Free from God's table.*
> *Come eat, come drink,*
> *Turn away from the things that do not satisfy*
> *And give God your life.*
> *Seek God and you will find him.*
> *God can take the pain away and give you peace instead.*
> *Come...*

If you wish, you can play some quiet music in the background as you give the students their invitations. Ask class members to quietly read their invitations and to spend some time silently praying and thinking about what God is asking them to do in their own hearts and lives. After a few minutes, invite those who are willing to share about what God is saying to them. Challenge *each* student to identify three things that he or she should do in response to God's invitation. When you are ready to move on, say, **If God is asking you to do something, he will make a way for it to happen.**

Finish Line

Note:

Don't forget to distribute copies of the Portable Sanctuary to students before they go.

OPTION 1 (LITTLE PREP)

Think about being satisfied in God.

Distribute to students copies of "More Than Enough" (Reproducible 2), or show it as a projection. If possible, play for students the song "Enough" by Chris Tomlin. Give students the opportunity to reflect on the questions and to share their thoughts with the rest of the class as a testimony to God's work in their lives. If you are able to play "Enough," discuss the lyrics of the song. How does "Enough" connect with God's work in their lives and with the things you have studied today?

Close the session in prayer, thanking God for being more than enough to satisfy and meet the needs in our lives.

OPTION 2 (MORE PREP)

Participate in a provision activity.

Work with your students to plan and implement a way to raise funds or collect food for a local shelter or food pantry. Perhaps your class can wash cars or perform some other service to raise funds; or, maybe students can canvas the neighborhood to collect canned goods, or collect canned goods from church members the next few Sundays. After you have accumulated the funds or the food items, make arrangements for your students to deliver them to the shelter or pantry and to help distribute them, if possible.

Close the session in prayer, asking God to meet the physical needs of those you will be serving and to also open their hearts to his spiritual provision.

The Invitation

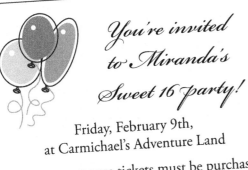

You're invited to Miranda's Sweet 16 party!

Friday, February 9th,
at Carmichael's Adventure Land

Discount entrance tickets must be purchased in advance at www.carmadven.com. Please log in under "Miranda's Party" when purchasing tickets. Cake and punch served at the main gate at 2 pm. Other food and drink not provided. Miranda is registered at Aurelia's, Vanish, and Marteen's.

Please RSVP with your ticket purchase by January 15th by calling or texting 555-3091.

You're invited to Melissa's Sweet 16 party!

Friday, February 9th,
at Lowen's World Class Resort

Activities provided all day, so come when you can. Activities include horseback riding, Frisbee golf, beach volleyball, swimming, kayaking, and surfing. Free food and drink all day. Transportation included.

Please RSVP by January 15th by calling or texting 555-0087.

Questions:

Which party offers activities that appeal to you more? _____

What surprises you about Melissa's invitation? About Miranda's? _____

_____

Which party would you most like to attend? Why? _____

_____

What would you recommend to Melissa and Miranda about how to improve their invitations?

_____

_____

More Than Enough

How has God been more than enough for you?

_____
_____
_____
_____

List some needs that God has met in your life.

_____
_____
_____
_____

How is God stretching you and growing you right now?

_____
_____
_____
_____

How can you share with others all that God means to you and all that God is doing in your life?

_____
_____
_____
_____

Portable Sanctuary

Day 1

Come to the Waters

Water is an amazing substance! It has qualities that we rarely ponder. For example, *cohesion* keeps water molecules together. You can't break water in its liquid form into pieces, even if you tried. It also has the quality of *adhesion*. It sticks to other molecules, which gives it the capability to move against gravity. If we didn't have water to drink, we would die. Water sustains us. Christ offers us water too—living water. What else could we count on to give us life?

Questions and Suggestions

- Read John 7:37–39. Why do you think Jesus used water as a metaphor for the life he gives?
- Have you experienced the presence of the Holy Spirit? Ask God to let his Spirit flow in you and through you like a stream of living water.

Day 2

Just Too Late

Have you ever been late for an airline flight? You had only seconds to spare, so you ran through the terminal, out of breath, hoping to make it. When you reached the counter, the airplane was already pulling out of the gate—the door closed, the airplane moving, and your seat already given away. At that point you would have taken *anything*—even being strapped to the wing or riding with the luggage! Think about how it feels when you realize that you're too late. What does it feel like for those who are too late to choose to follow God?

- How do you feel knowing that there is a time when God will be unapproachable? Are you ready to stand before God and give account of your life? Are your loved ones ready?
- Say a prayer for those who do not know Christ as Savior and Lord. Pray that God will give you chances to share about him.

Day 3
Searching for Fulfillment

The man had called himself the Messiah—the Christ. That was a shocking revelation, but even more shocking were his revelations about *her*. She had thought her first husband would love and value her, but he didn't—and neither did any of the next four husbands. Something was always missing. Since the commitment of marriage didn't seem to work, she was planning just to have a casual relationship with her current lover. There were no strings to tie either of them down, but even this relationship was not turning out as she hoped. But *this* man, the Christ, knew that—and he said that he had something to offer that would truly satisfy. Could she dare to hope?

Questions and Suggestions

- Read John 4:1–30, 39–42. What was the end result of the Samaritan woman's encounter with Christ?
- Imagine Jesus sitting and talking with you. Would he identify anything that you are trying to seek fulfillment from? Thank God that through Christ we can have more than enough—more than we'll ever need.

Day 4
Hard to Accept

For some it is much easier to give than to receive. Are you that kind of person? People who have a hard time receiving don't want to owe anything to anyone because they feel unworthy and undeserving. As a result, they fight against receiving. It is important to give, but it is

equally important to learn to graciously receive what others offer to us. God has given us the greatest gift—salvation. We should receive this gift with joy and thanksgiving.

Questions and Suggestions

- Have you ever been given a gift that was difficult to accept? What were the circumstances? Do you find it easier to give or receive? Why?
- This week, practice receiving gracefully.

Day 5
God's Ways

Eight-year-old Ha Eun was diagnosed with stomach cancer. After months of struggle, she was at the end of her life. Doctors fought just to keep her alive. Medicine had dissolved a large portion of the tumor but left her weak, with her organs shutting down. Many people were praying, and others trying to understand how God could let this happen to an innocent little girl. Then amazingly—and suddenly—Ha Eun's organs began to work again. Her little body got stronger and began to be healed. People were amazed, and some bowed at the feet of Jesus the Healer for the first time.

God's ways are not our ways, but we can stand in awe of God's power and love.

Questions and Suggestions

- Have you ever gotten angry or disillusioned with God because he did not do something the way you thought it should be done? What did you learn from that experience?
- Journal about some of "God's ways" that you have experienced in your life.

UNIT TWO

INTRO

Righteous Requirements

If you finally visit the Grand Canyon in person after only seeing it in pictures before, you'll be blown away by the view. What you'll finally see is the *panorama*—an unobstructed and complete view in all directions. A picture gives you only a part of what's going on, but you'll never get the full impact if you don't see the whole thing in person.

Session 1 starts this unit with a panoramic view of God's requirements for righteous living. The remaining sessions get specific with this: Session 2 touches on the remnant of people who passionately pursue God's righteousness, Session 3 focuses on the hope that the righteous have in God, Session 4 explores the worthlessness of religion without righteousness, and Session 5 examines the promise that God will be found by those who sincerely seek him.

When we take in the panorama of God's righteous requirements, we can finally begin to get the full picture of what God expects.

Unit 2 Special Prep

SESSION 1—WARM UP, Option 1 (Little Prep), calls for an offering receptacle. Option 2 (More Prep) requires time to tour your meeting place; you can also make some modifications to your meeting place. HOME STRETCH, Option 1 (Younger Youth), calls for hot dogs or dog or cat food. FINISH LINE, Option 2 (More Prep), requires some items of high value to display.

SESSION 2—WARM UP, Option 2 (More Prep), calls for a flame source and some objects to burn. FINISH LINE, Option 1 (Little Prep), requires some small index cards. Option 2 (More Prep) calls for a physical activity or service project that you and your students can complete together.

SESSION 3—For WARM UP, Option 1 (Little Prep), you can use candy or another small prize. Option 2 (More Prep) requires one or more large, soft rubber balls and room to play Dodge Ball; you can also use candy or other small prizes. STARTING LINE, Option 1 (Younger Youth), calls for some random books. For THE TURN you can use the audio and lyrics to the Chris Tomlin song "Famous One." FINISH LINE, Option 2 (More Prep), requires a helium tank, balloons, note cards, a hole punch, and yarn or ribbon.

SESSION 4—WARM UP, Option 2 (More Prep), calls for equipment to take and display a picture. STARTING LINE, Option 2 (Older Youth), requires computer and Internet access either before or during class time. HOME STRETCH, Option 1 (Younger Youth), calls for the information necessary to conduct a toy drive or similar collection effort. Option 2 (Older Youth) requires butcher paper and colored markers. FINISH LINE, Option 2 (More Prep), calls for a visit to an abandoned church, building, or neighborhood.

SESSION 5—For WARM UP, Option 1 (Little Prep), you can use the Digital BRIDGES CD, a computer, and a printer prior to class time. Option 2 (More Prep) requires an episode of the Andy Griffith show and the necessary equipment to watch it. STARTING LINE, Option 1 (Younger Youth), calls for envelopes; you can also use an elaborate turban and robe or other costume. FINISH LINE, Option 2 (More Prep), requires seeds for tomatoes, squash, or other plants and a place and time to plant and tend the seeds.

Leading into the Session

Warm Up

Option 1 Take an offering.
LITTLE PREP *Offering receptacle*

Option 2 Discover something "new."
MORE PREP *Time to tour your meeting place; modifications to meeting place (optional)*

Starting Line

Option 1 Discuss important things.
YOUNGER YOUTH *Chalkboard or dry erase board*

Option 2 Take a look at your culture.
OLDER YOUTH *Chalkboard or dry erase board*

Leading through the Session

Straight Away

Explore the Bible passages.
Bibles, Reproducible 1, pens or pencils

The Turn

Talk about the joy of discovering.

Leading beyond the Session

Home Stretch

Option 1 Analyze hot dogs or pet food.
YOUNGER YOUTH *Bible; hot dogs or dog or cat food*

Option 2 Discuss the purpose of sacrifice.
OLDER YOUTH *Chalkboard or dry erase board*

Finish Line

Option 1 Put justice, mercy, and humility into action.
LITTLE PREP *Reproducible 2, pens or pencils*

Option 2 Put your sacrifice into perspective.
MORE PREP *Bible, items of high value to display*

KNOWING WHAT IS GOOD

Bible Passages
Micah 3:1–4; 6:6–8

Key Verse
What does the LORD require of you? To act justly and to love mercy and to walk humbly with your God.
—Micah 6:8

Main Thought
God calls us to worship him in attitudes and actions.

Bible Background

The name *Micah* is a shortened form of two Hebrew words that mean "Who is like Yahweh?" Like Amos, Hosea, and Isaiah, Micah prophesied in the eighth century BC during the reigns of the Judahite kings Jotham, Ahaz, and Hezekiah. Virtually nothing is known of Micah's life, except that he came from the village of Moresheth-Gath in southwest Judah. Micah prophesied in and to the southern kingdom, seeing only the destruction of Jerusalem with no hope of deliverance. These prophecies placed him squarely in opposition to the ruling ideology of the day. Many of the city's leaders, including the royal court preachers, interpreted God's covenant with David (cf. 2 Sam 7:8–16) to mean that Jerusalem was invulnerable to attack or harm of any kind. The covenant with David became the foundation of a royal theology that blended religion with ideology to create a belief that David's successors would reign forever in Jerusalem—and if Jerusalem was safe, then so, ran the ideology, was Judah.

Micah neither believed in nor accepted the royal ideology. On the contrary, he dared to assert the unthinkable: Jerusalem would fall. Micah insisted that Torah obedience yields both righteousness and justice—right relationship with God and one's neighbor. Disaster awaited any people who failed to pursue justice and righteousness, even the people of God who lived in the great city of Jerusalem.

Micah 3:1–2 refers to the "rulers of the house of Israel," the ruling elite of Jerusalem, who "tear the skin from my people" and "who eat my people's flesh." This figurative language referred to a very serious situation. The political, religious, and financial rulers of Israel were using bribery and extortion to wrest money from the poor and common people. This utter lack of justice Micah ferociously turned into the grounds for destruction: "Zion will be plowed like a field, Jerusalem will become a heap of rubble, the temple hill a mound overgrown with thickets" (3:12).

Micah 6:6–8 is one of the high watermarks of Old Testament ethical monotheism: the One God requires justice and requires his people to live ethically according to Torah. Theodore of Mopsuestia, a theologian of the late fourth and early fifth century, wrote of Micah's call: "Forget about burnt offerings, countless sacrifices and oblations of firstborn, he [Micah] is saying. If you are concerned to appease the divinity, practice what God ordered you in the beginning through Moses. What in fact is that? To deliver fair judgment and decision in all cases where you have to choose better from worse, to continue giving evidence of all possible love and fellow-feeling to your neighbor, and be ready to put into practice what is pleasing to God in every way. He means, in short, 'You will love God with all your heart, all your mind, all your soul, and you will love your neighbor as yourself,' as was said of old through Moses. Do this, he is saying, as something preferable to sacrifices in God's eyes."[1]

1. Quoted in *Ancient Commentary on Scripture: Old Testament, vol. XIV, The Twelve Prophets,* ed. by Alberto Ferreiro (Downer's Grove: InterVarsity Press, 2003), 171–172.

OPTION 1 (LITTLE PREP)

Take an offering.

Begin the session by asking your students to contribute an offering, to you, in return for your faithful, quality teaching each week. Pass around a receptacle (such as an offering plate, a bucket, or even a baseball cap) into which students can place their offering. You will probably find that many of your students have no money on them, or that they suspect you are up to something (as usual). After the receptacle has been around, pass it again, and ask that each student contribute something of value, even if it's not money. This time you may get some assorted pocket contents, jewelry, or shoes.

Tally up your collection, return everything to the original owners, and say, **I am touched by your offering—but your presence in class each week is enough "offering" for me.**

Warm Up

Note:

If you sent the Portable Sanctuary home with students last week, take some time at the beginning of this session to review and discuss their experience.

• •

OPTION 2 (MORE PREP)

Discover something "new."

Divide students into small groups and allow a few minutes for the groups to explore the church (or meeting place). The groups should seek to discover new things about the church (or meeting place)—things they have not seen or noticed before or rooms they have never been in. If you wish, you can purposely make some modifications or changes to some of the rooms that your students are already familiar with and see if anyone notices. After the groups return, ask each to share what they noticed and why they think they never noticed it before.

Say, **When we do some exploring, we can discover new things—and some things that were there all along.**

OPTION 1 (YOUNGER YOUTH)

Discuss important things.

Say, **I'm going to name some different things in life and I want you to tell me why each of them is important.** Begin by writing some obvious things on the board and invite students to respond to each:

Starting Line

- *God* (God made us and everything in the universe; we depend on God for life.)
- *Church* (The church is God's hands and feet on earth, the people of God.)
- *Family* (Our family provides for our basic needs and cares for us.)
- *School* (School gives us the knowledge we need to succeed in the world.)

Continue by listing some other things whose importance is not as obvious:

- *Music* (Music can allow us to worship, help us to learn, and provide enjoyment for our lives.)

- *Starbucks* (This type of place provides an atmosphere for fellowship and relaxation.)
- *The Internet* (This is a primary tool for information gathering, education, and communication.)
- *Sports* (Participating in sports helps to keep us physically fit and brings enjoyment to our lives.)

Feel free to add any other things that might be pertinent to your students' lives. The point is not to rank these things in importance, but to show that even fun and enjoyable things can be important to our lives.

When you are ready to move on, say, **Let's take a look at some of the things that are important to God.**

. . . .

OPTION 2 (OLDER YOUTH)
Take a look at your culture.

Help your students to think about the use of worship in our society by discussing the following questions:

- **What does it mean to *worship* something?** *Worship* means to give reverence, respect, admiration, or devotion to something.
- **What things do people worship other than God?** People worship other people, themselves, money, popularity, possessions, certain lifestyles, and so forth. If you look at what a person spends time and money on and shows enthusiasm about, then you will know what is truly important to that person.
- **How does worship affect the person or thing being worshiped? How does it affect the one doing the worshiping?** An inanimate object is not affected at all by worship. (God pointed out frequently in the Old Testament that it is silly to worship a dead stone or a chunk of wood.) A person who is worshiped can become quite conceited by all the praise that he or she receives. The people who do the worshiping can feel satisfied if they think they are doing the right thing; they can also become addicted to the act of worship or dependent on it as a perceived way to receive satisfaction or some other benefit.

When you are ready to move on, say, **Let's take a look at just what we should offer to God in worship.**

Explore the Bible passages.

Distribute to students copies of "The Best Offering" (Reproducible 1). Read together Micah 3:1–4 and 6:6–8 and discuss the following questions, encouraging students to use the handout as a study guide:

Straight Away

- **Does anyone really hate good and love evil? Explain.** Invite students to respond. Point out that when people take a stand for godly values, for the family, for marriage, or for the unborn, they are often met by angry words, profanity, and ridicule. In today's society, many people seem to enjoy the "shock value" of doing the wildest stuff they can, while condemning anyone who claims Christ and actually acts like it. It is certainly true that some people actively embrace evil while attacking or poking fun at good.

- **Were these people from Israel cannibals? What is all this talk about tearing skin, breaking bones, and eating flesh?** Micah used striking visual terms to illustrate what God's people had been doing; their treatment of others was an embarrassment to God, so harsh that Micah compared it to murder.

- **Are there any people today who act this way while claiming the name of God? Explain.** Invite students to respond. Point out that this passage was addressed to leaders. People in positions of power have a responsibility to use that power wisely and fairly. At times wars have been (and are) fought and people killed in the name of God. Spiritual leaders in the church are entrusted by God with the care of others' souls. These leaders have the potential to do much damage if they're not careful. Your students may be familiar with recent molestation scandals in the Catholic church and other church groups.

- **How did Micah indicate that God would respond to these leaders?** He said that God will not answer their cries. Challenge your students to consider the possibility that there are times when God might not respond to us. In this case, the people's actions did not indicate that their cries to God were sincere. Also, we know that when we choose to treat others harshly, then we can expect to suffer the consequences of our actions.

- **God had specifically asked the Israelites to sacrifice to him—burnt offerings of calves and rams. Much of Exodus, Leviticus, Numbers, and Deuteronomy detail the specifics of God's requirements and describe the Israelites making these sacrifices. Yet here, God seems to have been rejecting these sacrifices. Why? What was God looking for?** God said that the people were just "going through the motions" of the sacrifices. Their "church life" was not consistent with the way they treated others during the rest of the week. Instead of precisely following the rules of cooking a cow, God would rather see us show justice and mercy to others and be humble (not proud or arrogant) in our conduct.

- **What are some things we do for or with God that may become simply "going through the motions" for us? How does this happen?** Invite students to respond. Many people are pumped up when they start attending a new church or when a new pastor comes, but over time—gradually— they lose their motivation. Even prayer, Bible study, and serving others can become routine for us if our hearts are not in it. When we fail to really think about what we're doing or to pause and reflect on what we've experienced, we can fall into a rut. This is why camps and conventions get people stirred up—and why the excitement often does not last.

- **What attempt at "extreme worship" did Micah describe here? How do we sometimes do the same thing?** See 6:7, where Micah talked about sacrificing thousands of rams, ten thousand rivers of oil, and even giving one's own firstborn child as a sacrifice! These people were trying to make it all better with God by "doing church" more, but God was looking for something else. We sometimes do similar things—for example, a person sins, feels bad, and then tries to "make up for it" by praying more, reading the Bible more, and going to church more, when God will forgive if we simply ask with a repentant heart. Some people even give large financial gifts to the church because it makes them feel better or because they think God will bless them for it.

- **God *requires* us "to act justly and to love mercy and to walk humbly with … God" (6:8). How does this compare to all the sacrificial requirements from Exodus, Leviticus, Numbers, and Deuteronomy?** *Require* is a powerful word; it makes most of us think of obligations placed on us to do certain things that lead us to a goal—we are required to pass our classes to graduate, we are required to take driver's education to get a driver's license, and so forth. But God did not lay down laws here—he told us how to live, who to be, the way to go on our journey in life. Micah 6:8 is not a checklist to go through to please God; it's a way of being that touches every part of our lives—in church and out.

Say, **Our character is an important part of our relationship with God.**

The Turn

Talk about the joy of discovering.
Ask the following questions to explore how your students feel about discovery:

- **Would you rather spend a warm Saturday in front of the television or exploring the woods behind your friend's house?**
- **Would you rather spend the evening listening to your favorite CDs or checking out some new artists whom you have heard about?**
- **Would you rather reread a favorite book or start on one you have never read before?**

You can have students break into small groups to discuss these questions or else go through them together. Ask any students who do not resonate with any of these "adventures" to name their own favorite types of discovery.

Explain that discovering is a wonderful and exciting part of life—discovering new music, discovering a new book, discovering new friends, and the list could go on and on. In order to discover it is necessary for us to move forward, to try something unfamiliar. Usually, discovery means we find something that was already there. Pirates discover treasure that has been buried by someone else. When someone poured hot water over some ground-up beans from Ethiopia and called it coffee, that person was simply finding a new way to use something that was already there. Through the words of Micah, the Israelites discovered something that was already there—God's desire for them to live just, merciful, and humble lives.

Say, **God invites us to discover what is good and what he requires of us.**

OPTION 1 (YOUNGER YOUTH)

Analyze hot dogs or pet food.

Bring to class some hot dogs and/or some pet food. It is up to you how fancy you get with this; you could simply bring these things in the package or can or actually cook some hot dogs and prepare them to serve to your students.

As you study the hot dogs and/or pet food or eat the hot dogs, ask, **Do you know what's in this stuff?** Hot dogs can contain pork, beef, chicken, turkey, or a combination of these. Sometimes even the snouts, beaks, ears, and organs of the animals are ground up and included with the meat. Pet food can contain ground parts of the meat carcass such as necks, feet, bones, heads, and intestines. Sometimes the animals used to make pet food have been rejected for human consumption because they were dead, dying, diseased, or disabled. If your students were unaware of this, it is not likely that they will ever view hot dogs (or pet food) the same way again. It is also not likely that they will ever forget this session! Refer students back to Micah 3:1–4. Point out that the grisly reality of hot dogs and/or pet food is very similar to Micah's description of the behavior of ancient Israel's leaders.

When you are ready to move on, say, **God calls us to be people of justice and mercy, not people who trample on others.**

Home Stretch

Website:

See http://en.wikipedia.org/wiki/Hot_dog and http://en.wikipedia.org/wiki/Dog_food for more information.

OPTION 2 (OLDER YOUTH)

Discuss the purpose of sacrifice.

Write the word *sacrifice* on the board. Discuss the following questions:

• **Why do people sacrifice things?** As students respond, write their ideas on the board. To *sacrifice* something is to give it up. Sometimes we sacrifice involuntarily (as when someone wakes us up early and we lose our precious sleep). Sometimes we sacrifice for our own benefit (as when we give up money in exchange for a product or a service). Sometimes we sacrifice for the benefit of others (as when parents give up things they want in order to provide for their kids). And sometimes we sacrifice spontaneously, as when we give our worship as an offering to God.

• **What sorts of things do we have to sacrifice in order to maintain a relationship with God?** Invite students to respond. Journeying with God involves a commitment of time and effort on our part, it means setting our own agendas aside to seek God and to serve others, and it means we might not do certain things or hang out with certain people because of our love for the Lord.

• **What might it look like in your life to do justice, to love mercy, and to walk humbly with God?** Invite students to respond. These aspects of our God-relationship are all carried out in our interaction with others. God calls us to treat everyone with fairness and mercy, but to do so quietly, without calling attention to ourselves.

When you are ready to move on, say, **The sacrifice God calls for is a sacrifice of our attitudes and actions.**

Finish Line

Note:

Don't forget to distribute copies of the Portable Sanctuary to students before they go.

OPTION 1 (LITTLE PREP)

Put justice, mercy, and humility into action.

Distribute copies of "Action Plan" (Reproducible 2) or show it as a projection. Go over the instructions and give students time to work on the handout alone, in pairs, or in small groups. After a few minutes, bring everyone back together and invite students to share their ideas. Emphasize for each area the connection between the worship of God and the treatment of others, and the positive effect that our actions and attitudes have on our relationship with God. Encourage your students to share about additional areas of their lives where they can be humble agents of God's justice and mercy. There are plenty of people in the world and in our lives who have been ground up and beaten down by others, and they are longing for the justice and mercy that God gives through us.

Close the session in prayer, remembering any special needs in your group and asking God to continue to teach your students what is good and what he requires of their lives.

OPTION 2 (MORE PREP)

Put your sacrifice into perspective.

Bring to class some items of high value to display. Try to bring a combination of things that are valuable in their own right (such as a diamond ring, an expensive watch, an expensive cell phone, and so forth) and things that have personal sentimental value (such as your wedding picture, a drawing your kid made, a memento from a special event, and so forth). Explain what each item is and what it is worth. For the sentimental items, provide extra detail about why those things mean so much to you. Point out that you or others sacrificed greatly in order for you to have these things. Now, read aloud Romans 8:31–32: **"What, then, shall we say in response to this? If God is for us, who can be against us? He who did not spare his own Son, but gave him up for us all—how will he not also, along with him, graciously give us all things?"** Say, **God sacrificed the One of greatest worth and closest to his heart for our sakes. What could we possibly sacrifice in return except for our own lives?**

Close the session in prayer, remembering any special needs in your group and asking God to continue to teach your students what is good and what he requires of their lives.

The Best Offering

Read Micah 3:1–4 and 6:6–8, looking for answers to the following questions.

• Does anyone really hate good and love evil? Explain. _____
_____
_____

• Were these people from Israel cannibals? What is all this talk about tearing skin, breaking bones, and eating flesh? _____
_____
_____

• Are there any people today who act this way while claiming the name of God? Explain.
_____
_____
_____

• How did Micah indicate that God would respond to these leaders? _____
_____
_____

• God had specifically asked the Israelites to sacrifice to him—burnt offerings of calves and rams. Much of Exodus, Leviticus, Numbers, and Deuteronomy detail the specifics of God's requirements and describe the Israelites making these sacrifices. Yet here, God seems to have been rejecting these sacrifices. Why? What was God looking for? _____
_____
_____

• What are some things we do for or with God that may become simply "going through the motions" for us? How does this happen? _____
_____
_____

• What attempt at "extreme worship" did Micah describe here? How do we sometimes do the same thing?
_____
_____
_____

• God *requires* us to "act justly and to love mercy, and to walk humbly with … God" (6:8). How does this compare to all the sacrificial requirements from Exodus, Leviticus, Numbers, and Deuteronomy?
_____
_____
_____

Action Plan

If we do not live as humble people of justice and mercy, we are like composite hot dogs or Grade A dog food. The powerful principles of Micah 3:1–4 and 6:6–8 are just empty words if we don't put them into action.

Think about some places and some ways where you can act justly, love mercy, and walk humbly with God:

• In your personal times with God. _____

• In and through your church. _____

• In your family. _____

• In your school. _____

• In the music you listen to. _____

• At Starbucks. _____

• When using the Internet. _____

• When playing sports. _____

• Others _____

_____

_____

_____

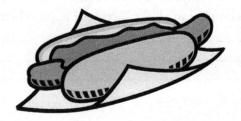

Portable Sanctuary

Day 1

Discovering a Little More of Me

Read 1 John 3:1–3, in *The Message* Bible if possible. Whatever translation you use, read it the first time *slowly*. Now read it again, but this time really pay attention to what you are reading. Enjoy the words instead of rushing through them. Now go back through the text again and put yourself into it. Picture the words being spoken directly to you, specifically about you. God speaks to us through the Word. It is a living and active book, able to pierce us to our very souls (Hebrews 4:12).

Questions and Suggestions

- What is God saying to you through his Word? Write out what you feel God is calling you to do.
- This week, spend some time in the Word every day. How does this touch your life?
- Pray.

Day 2

Daily Reflection

Grab a newspaper, watch the evening news, or check out an Internet news service such as www.foxnews.com or www.cnn.com. Check the headlines and look for stories of right and wrong. Now think back on your day yesterday. What happened that was right or wrong? Did you see a good deed or an act of kindness? What were some good things you observed either in other people or in your own life? What resulted from what you saw or experienced? God has shown you what is good and what God requires of you. Did what you experienced yesterday, or saw yesterday, reflect what God has shown you?

N O T E S

Questions and Suggestions

- Read Micah 6:6–8. What are some situations in your life where you are trying to figure out what is right and what is wrong? Who might help you to know what to do?
- Who and what did God create you to be? What do you need to do about it?
- Pray.

Day 3
The Journey of Youth

When we journey with God he brings deep joy to our lives—not the joy of an easy life or of no responsibilities but the joy of purpose and presence. God gives us a purpose that gets us outside of our self-centeredness and takes us beyond our comfort zones, and God's presence with us assures us that his purpose for us will be accomplished. When you leave it in God's hands and seek to do the things that God asks, you will experience a joy that nothing else in life can give.

Questions and Suggestions

- Read Ecclesiastes 11:9–10. How does it feel to think about God bringing you to judgment? What can you do to be ready for that day?
- Start each day by asking God to direct you in paths of justice and mercy.
- Pray.

Day 4
Discovering New Hope

In his book *A Cup of Coffee at the Soul Café* (Nashville: Broadman & Holman Publishers, 1998), Leonard Sweet quotes Eugene Peterson as saying, "Hope is a response to the future, which has its foundations in the promises of God. It looks at the future as time for the completion of God's promise.... Christian hope alerts us to the possibilities of the future as a field of action, and as a consequence, fills the present with energy" (87). In other words, our hope in the future dictates how we live *now*.

Questions and Suggestions

- Read Romans 15:13. What are you hoping for your future? How could walking humbly with God influence your hope?
- What things bring hope to your life? How can you give hope to others?
- Pray.

Day 5
God's Tattoo for Us

Today, people get tattoos as fashion statements—as something to make them "look cool," to draw attention to themselves, or to express something about who they are. Tattoos have also been used to indicate ownership, although we know now that people do not "belong" to other people. But God marks our lives with grace and blessing—as a sign that we are his, and as an invitation to others to thank and enjoy the Lord. God's mark on our lives does not so much indicate *who* we are as it indicates whose we are.

Questions and Suggestions

- Read Psalm 67 (from *The Message* Bible, if possible). How has God's mark on you changed your life?
- How is your smile? Do others see it much? Do *you* see it much? Remember to thank God with every breath and to enjoy God at all times.
- Pray.

Leading into the Session

Warm Up

Option 1 Pit the lions against the wolves.
LITTLE PREP *Paper, pens or pencils, chalkboard or dry erase board*

Option 2 Conduct a fire experiment.
MORE PREP *Flame source, various objects to burn*

Starting Line

Option 1 Remember the oppressors.
YOUNGER YOUTH

Option 2 Talk about the unexpected.
OLDER YOUTH

Leading through the Session

Straight Away

Explore the Bible passage.
Bibles

The Turn

Seek the bigger picture.
Bibles, Reproducible 1, pens or pencils

Leading beyond the Session

Home Stretch

Option 1 Discuss serving shoulder to shoulder.
YOUNGER YOUTH *Bible, paper, pens or pencils*

Option 2 Apply the passage.
OLDER YOUTH *Reproducible 2, pens or pencils*

Finish Line

Option 1 Pick and choose.
LITTLE PREP *Small index cards, pens or pencils*

Option 2 Work shoulder to shoulder.
MORE PREP *A physical activity or service project*

SESSION 2

THE RIGHTEOUS REMNANT

Bible Passage
Zephaniah 3:1–13

Key Verse
The remnant of Israel will do no wrong.
—Zephaniah 3:13

Main Thought
God preserves a remnant of people who pursue his righteousness.

Bible Background

In the Hebrew Bible the "Book of the Twelve" contains the writings of the so-called "minor prophets" (those other than Isaiah, Jeremiah, and Ezekiel). In the Book of the Twelve we find Amos, Hosea, Micah, and Zephaniah, among others. Given the content of his book, Zephaniah is thought to have preached during the reign of Josiah and probably before the reform of 621 BC. Josiah was the boy king who ascended to the throne in Jerusalem in the wake of a palace coup against his father Amon, who had continued the downward moral and religious slide begun by his father Manasseh. Under Manasseh the people of Jerusalem had abandoned the reform of King Hezekiah and had sunk so far as to erect symbols of the Canaanite gods Baal and Asherah and altars for their worship in the temple itself. Manasseh's rule represented the low point in the history of the kings of Judah.

Since Josiah was still a boy when he became king a regency was established to guide his decisions. In the early years of his reign it was still an open question which way Jerusalem and Judah would go. Would they return to the worship of God alone or sink further into religious syncretism? In 621 BC Josiah led a thorough reform of the nation's religious life, ordering the removal of every vestige of Baal worship. Despite that reform the wickedness of the previous kings was so profound that "the LORD did not turn away from the heat of his fierce anger, which burned against Judah because of all that Manasseh had done to provoke him to anger" (2 Kings 23:26). It was this anger that fueled the prophecy of Zephaniah.

The prophets who were active in Jerusalem and Judah before the Babylonian invasion and the subsequent exile in 589 BC had common themes to their preaching. Thus we find in Zephaniah oracles or sayings about the Day of the Lord as a time of judgment and not light, burning indictments of the people of God for their sins against God and neighbor, even God's judgments against nations other than Israel and Judah. Chapter 3 contains many of these themes in a remarkably condensed package.

Despite the presence of God in their very midst the religious and political leadership of Judah persisted in wrongdoing. Jerusalem was portrayed as the "city of oppressors" (3:1). Through religious rituals and observances such as the Passover and other festivals, Israel would have recalled the days when they lived as an oppressed people in Egypt, "the house of bondage." The Egyptians had been Israel's *oppressors*—and now Zephaniah applied that same word to the Jerusalem leadership in a stinging rebuke of policies that ground down their own people. Like ravenous predators, political and religious leaders had conspired against the powerless, leaving them without a shred of anything to call their own. In the midst of this evil, however, God dispensed justice. This chilling reminder was a warning that God will not be mocked forever. Judgment was coming, said Zephaniah. Perhaps surprisingly, given this harsh warning, verses 9–10 held out the most striking promise of restoration, a time when all peoples would serve God in peace and solidarity with one another and the Lord.

OPTION 1 (LITTLE PREP)

Pit the lions against the wolves.

Divide the class into groups based on criteria of your choosing (by age, by school, by height, or by something totally random). Distribute paper and pens or pencils to group members and invite them to discuss a hypothetical battle between lions and wolves. Which do they think would win? Why? What are the characteristics of each that would be of benefit in battle? What would a cross between a lion and a wolf be called (think of Napoleon Dynamite's *liger*)? What would it look like? Groups should record their thoughts and ideas. After a few minutes, invite the groups to discuss their ideas with the rest of the class as you take notes on the board. Lions definitely have the size and strength advantage, but wolves are faster and can run for longer spans of time. Point out that both species are predatory carnivores—that is, they hunt other animals and eat them as their primary food source.

Say, **Lions and wolves would have no problem tearing you to shreds for a meal.**

OPTION 2 (MORE PREP)

Conduct a fire experiment.

Bring to class a flame source and some various objects you can burn. Your flame source could be as mild as a book of matches or as potent as a propane torch; objects to burn might include paper, pencils, sticks, and even a small piece of furniture. Purposely include some things that will not burn with your flame (rocks, metal objects, and so forth). Make sure you have a safe and suitable location to burn the objects—isolated, well-ventilated, and away from smoke detectors and other objects. Seek the permission of your church or host home before doing this option, and use your common sense about what you burn and where and how you burn it.

Start by burning the smallest and most flammable objects, one at a time. As you move on to larger or nonflammable items, ask, **Do you think *this* will burn?** Point out that with enough heat applied, *anything* can be consumed or destroyed—even rocks and metal will melt or decompose into their component elements. Ask, **Why do we sometimes call an insult "burning" someone?** Cruel words or actions hurt, like a flame hurts.

Say, **It doesn't feel good to be "burned" or to be consumed by someone else's anger.**

Warm Up

Note:

If you sent the Portable Sanctuary home with students last week, take some time at the beginning of this session to review and discuss their experience.

Web site:

To find more specifics about lions and wolves, see http://en.wikipedia.org/wiki/Lion and http://en.wikipedia.org/wiki/Gray_wolf.

Starting Line

Note:

Be sensitive to any students who might currently be the victims of bullying.

OPTION 1 (YOUNGER YOUTH)

Remember the oppressors.

Say, **I want you to tell me about the biggest bully you knew in grade school. Invite students to share about their memories of bullies in school.** Share some memories of people who were bullies when you were in school. Now ask, **Why do these people act this way?** There is always some issue that drives a bully to oppress others (hurt them with his or her power)—neglect or abuse at home, inadequacy in other areas (social or academic), or something else. Bullies often have a size or strength advantage that they use to hurt or control others. Ask, **Whatever happened to the bullies you knew?** Sometimes these people get their issues solved before they grow up. If they don't, they end up as dysfunctional adults, sometimes in trouble with the law. Point out that it is never pleasant to be oppressed by someone else.

When you are ready to move on, say, **Let's see what God said about people who oppress others.**

OPTION 2 (OLDER YOUTH)

Talk about the unexpected.

Share any or all of the following stories with your class:

- **A Finnish opera singer was injured while cycling when a squirrel ran into his bicycle spokes and flipped his bike. The singer suffered a broken nose in the fall. This goes to prove the age-old theory: squirrels hate opera.** *(Relevant Magazine,* Issue 23, Nov–Dec 2006, p 34).
- **One time when I was a kid, I fell out of the tree that I climbed daily. It hurt. I had climbed the tree hundreds of times without incident. I was surprised I fell.** (the author)
- **I worked at my first job out of college for three years. One day, out of the blue, my boss called me in and threatened to fire me. This was a total surprise because I saw him every day, and he had never said anything bad about my work.** (the editor)

Feel free to add some stories of your own about being surprised or experiencing the unexpected. Invite students to talk about the unexpected by discussing the following questions:

- **Have you ever been totally surprised by something? Describe the experience.**
- **What is the biggest surprise you have experienced this week? How about today?**
- **Have you ever been surprised by something God did or didn't do? How did you feel? What did you learn?**

Point out that the unexpected can be a positive thing (such as a surprise gift) or a negative thing (such as a sudden illness). By its very nature, something unexpected catches us by surprise—we are not expecting it and are not necessarily prepared for it.

When you are ready to move on, say, **Let's see how God's people received some unexpected news from him.**

Straight Away

Leading through the Session

Explore the Bible passage.

Read together Zephaniah 3:1–13. Discuss the following questions:

- **Has anyone heard of King Josiah from the Old Testament? Do you know what he was famous for?** Josiah became king of Judah when he was just eight years old. Josiah's father and grandfather had been evil and corrupt kings, but Josiah was passionately devoted to the Lord. Explain that this passage was likely written when Josiah was king.

- **Who was Zephaniah talking about here? What pointed words did he use to describe their terrible acts?** Zephaniah was addressing the people of "the city" (vv 1, 7, and 11). Explain that the people would have easily recognized this as referring to the capital city of Jerusalem. This is clarified in verse 13, which addresses "the remnant of Israel." The people were called oppressors, disobedient, distrustful, lions and wolves, arrogant and treacherous, profane and violent, shameless, corrupt, proud, and haughty. These are not flattering terms! The word *oppressors* would have called to mind the Egyptians, who had oppressed the Israelites as slaves for many years. This was a powerful statement about the corruption and evil that had happened in among God's people.

- ***Within*** **Judah and the city, who were these words addressed to? What do these people have in common?** Zephaniah addressed the government officials, the prophets, and the priests. These were the leaders of the people. Those who had the greatest power—and the responsibility to care for the rest of the population—were doing a terrible job.

- **If someone gave you a description of your life—a terrible but accurate description—and then you learned that it was God who gave the description, how would you respond?** You would probably be embarrassed and scared. You might cry, pray, look for help, try to change, and plead with God for patience and mercy. This is just what Josiah and the people did (see 2 Kings 23).

- **How did Zephaniah expand the application of these words beyond just the people of Judah?** He pointed out that God had destroyed other nations because of their corruption and disobedience, and that Judah should have learned a lesson from this (vv 6–7). God's anger would be so fierce that it would consume the entire world (v 8).

- **What good would come from all of this?** The people would be purified, call upon the Lord, and serve him together (v 9); the proud would be removed and the humble would remain (vv 11–12); there would be a remnant (smaller, surviving portion of the former group) who would do the right thing (v 13).

- **Zephaniah talked of a remnant of people who would do no wrong, speak no lies, and live in peace. How would these people be able to do this?** Look at verse 9. The wrath and punishment of God woke the people up, and the *purifying action of God* made the people holy. Explain that we are called to respond to God, but it is God who does the work and makes the change in us.

- **Josiah was a godly king (see 2 Kings 23). Why would Zephaniah speak all these words of God's wrath during the reign of a godly king?** Refer students to 2 Kings 22:14–20. There were still consequences to the evil that had been done prior to Josiah's reign. However, these consequences were delayed because of Josiah's commitment to God. Point out that making a decision to follow God does not remove the consequences of poor decisions we have made before (or might make in the future).

Say, **God preserved a remnant of people in Josiah's time who pursued God's righteousness.**

The Turn

Seek the bigger picture.

Distribute to students copies of "The Bigger Picture" (Reproducible 1) or show it as a projection. Students can work on the handout alone, in pairs or small groups, or all together. After a few minutes, bring everyone together and invite them to share their responses. Here are some ideas to stimulate your students' thinking:

- Any time we take advantage of our power (over people who are weaker, poorer, smaller, younger, or less smart than we are), we are oppressive.
- Many people in our society and world who have power (over people who are weaker, poorer, smaller, younger, or less smart than we are) are oppressive. They won't take advice from anyone, they care nothing about seeking God, they take everything they can get, they are proud, and they think they live above the law.
- Every city/town, school, church, family, and individual needs the help and intervention of God. Challenge your students to identify the real needs around them and within them, to consider whether those people are seeking God's help, and to think about what they could be doing.

Say, **God is looking *today* for a remnant of people who will pursue God's righteousness.**

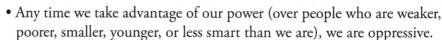

Leading beyond the Session

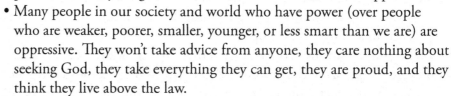

Home Stretch

OPTION 1 (YOUNGER YOUTH)

Discuss serving shoulder to shoulder.

Read again Zephaniah 3:9: "Then will I purify the lips of the peoples, that all of them may call on the name of the LORD and serve him shoulder to shoulder." Ask, **What images come to mind when you think about serving shoulder to shoulder?** This makes us think of working closely with others, of working toward a common goal, of helping others with the job—I share your burden, you share my burden, we all share one another's burdens and move forward on our journey with God.

Divide the class into groups by school, by age, or by some other criterion of your choosing. Appoint one leader per group, distribute paper and pens or pencils, and give the groups time to brainstorm about working shoulder to shoulder. How do they see this happening—and how could it happen—in the following areas? Some possible answers are given:

- *Your school:* Schools are usually comprised of *cliques*—groups of people that each share similar interests or characteristics. If these groups would interact and share openly with one another, no one would be left out—and everyone would learn and gain from the experience.
- *The churches of your community:* Many churches are duplicating their efforts, trying to do the same things for the same people at the same time. If these churches would pool their resources and people to work together, they might get more done—and help more people.
- *Your own church:* Different groups in the church (youth, children's ministry, women's ministry, and so forth) sometimes follow their own agendas and don't interact much with one another. If these groups got together and worked for the same goals, they might be able to do more—and help more people.
- *Your own youth group:* Youth groups also sometimes develop cliques, making it hard for new people to fit in. A very small group can become so close that new people find it hard to connect, and a very large group can be so overwhelming that new people don't know *where* to fit in. In a youth group, "shoulder to shoulder" means that everyone is equal and is respected.

Feel free to add other categories based on the particular culture and needs of your youth. After a few minutes, invite the group leaders to share what their groups have come up with.

When you are ready to move on, say, **Pursuing God's righteousness means that we work, worship, and serve shoulder to shoulder with others.**

· ·

Option 2 (Older Youth)

Apply the passage.

Distribute to students copies of "The Great Turnaround" (Reproducible 2) or show it as a projection. Break the class into groups by school, by age, or by some other criterion of your choosing, and appoint one leader per group. Read aloud Zephaniah 3:9, 12–13 from *The Message* Bible:

> ⁹ **In the end I will turn things around for the people.**
> **I'll give them a language undistorted, unpolluted,**
> **Words to address   in worship**
> **and, united, to serve me with their shoulders to the wheel.**
> ¹² **I'll leave a core of people among you**
> **who are poor in spirit—**
> **What's left of Israel that's really Israel.**
> **They'll make their home in God.**
> ¹³ **This core holy people**
> **will not do wrong.**

They won't lie,
won't use words to flatter or seduce.
Content with who they are and where they are,
unanxious, they'll live at peace.

(*The Message* [MSG], Copyright © 1993, 1994, 1995, 1996, 2000, 2001, 2002 by Eugene H. Peterson)

Now invite group members to work together to interpret and apply these verses, one at a time. After groups are finished, bring them back together and invite the leaders to share their work. Some possible answers are as follows:

Verse 9

Interpretation—God is going to make things better. He will teach us how to worship and how to serve him together.

Application—We can have hope that God is working for the good. We need to investigate how God is leading and how we can work together for God.

Verse 12

Interpretation—No matter how many hypocrites we may see in the church, there are some faithful people in there. They are humble, the true church, and they fully rely on God.

Application—We can be a part of God's humble, sincere "core of people." This is what God is really looking for.

Verse 13

Interpretation—God's true followers live holy lives. They speak the truth, and they're not greedy. They don't live in worry or fear; they live in peace.

Application—God expects and enables us to live holy lives full of truth. Living this way in God is the only way we'll ever know peace.

Encourage your students that no matter where they have been, no matter where they are now, and no matter what things look like around them, God can turn things around and put them on a new path.

When you are ready to move on, say, **God wants *you* in the righteous core, serving him in righteousness and peace.**

Finish Line

Option 1 (Little Prep)

Pick and choose.

Distribute small index cards and pens or pencils to the class. Invite each student to reflect on the responses that were given during the HOME STRETCH activity and to write down on an index card his or her favorite idea, one that could be carried out in the coming days. Invite those who are willing to share which ideas they chose and why. Encourage students to keep their cards in a place where they will see them and be reminded to follow through.

Close the session in prayer, asking God to make your group a righteous remnant in the midst of your community.

Note: Don't forget to distribute copies of the Portable Sanctuary to students before they go.

OPTION 2 (MORE PREP)

Work shoulder to shoulder.

Before class, determine a physical activity or service project that your students can complete, in the name of the Lord, together. The idea is for class members to work shoulder to shoulder, not individually. Painting a structure, moving a heavy object, or even providing special music as a group for the congregation would work well. This should be a task that does not single out any one student and that cannot be completed effectively without shoulder-to-shoulder participation. Whether you are able to do this task at this time or need to schedule time outside of class to complete it, praise your students for serving shoulder to shoulder when they are through, and point out that each person's efforts were necessary.

Close the session in prayer, asking God to make your group a righteous remnant in the midst of your community.

> *Note:*
>
> Don't forget to distribute copies of the Portable Sanctuary to students before they go.

"I can't seem to get a strike to save my soul, but, fortunately, the salvation of my soul doesn't depend upon my getting a strike!"

The Bigger Picture

Read Zephaniah 3:1–5. At what times has this passage described you? When has it described your family, a friend, or someone else you know? What are the parallels between your world/culture/society and this passage? _____

_____

_____

_____

_____

Now read Zephaniah 3:8–9. To "wait" for the Lord means to stick close to him, to long for what is coming, to wait for God to act. In what ways are the following things waiting for the Lord? How do they need God's intervention and help? What are they doing about it?

• Your city/town _____

• Your school _____

• Your church _____

• Your family _____

• You _____

The Great Turnaround

Read Zephaniah 3:9, 12–13 below. How would you interpret or paraphrase these verses? How do they apply to the world today and to your life situation?

9   In the end I will turn things around for the people.
      I'll give them a language undistorted, unpolluted,
      Words to address GOD in worship
      and, united, to serve me with their shoulders to the wheel.

How would you interpret this verse?_____
_____

How would you apply this verse? _____
_____
_____

12 I'll leave a core of people among you
      who are poor in spirit—
      What's left of Israel that's really Israel.
      They'll make their home in GOD.

How would you interpret this verse? _____
_____

How would you apply this verse? _____
_____
_____

13 This core holy people
      will not do wrong.
      They won't lie,
      won't use words to flatter or seduce.
      Content with who they are and where they are,
      unanxious, they'll live at peace.

How would you interpret this verse? _____
_____

How would you apply this verse? _____
_____
_____

Portable Sanctuary

Day 1

Keep On Waiting

Have you ever waited for a phone call? What was the phone call for? Have you ever waited for a letter? What were you hoping it would contain? Much of life involves waiting. Once, when I went surfing, I waited all day for the "ultimate wave"—and it was well worth it. Three other times I waited for nine months—and my life changed for the better each time as I carried my newborn child home. The Bible encourages us to wait on the Lord. And the Bible tells us that God shows up. All the waiting brings us into an encounter with the God of the universe.

Questions and Suggestions

- Read Psalm 33:20–22. Spend some time with this passage. Rewrite it so that it reflects a personal perspective: "*I wait in hope for the Lord. . . .*"
- What are you waiting for in life? What *should* you be waiting for? What are you anticipating from God this week?
- Pray.

Day 2

One Matters

You are important. You matter. The power of one is amazing. In his book *AquaChurch* (Loveland, Colo: Group Publishing, 1999, 97–98), Leonard Sweet illustrates how much difference one can make: "In 1649, one vote caused Charles I of England to be executed. In 1776, one vote gave America the English language instead of German.

---

life to helping others—giving second chances, paying debts, blessing people. He gave beauty for ashes.

Questions and Suggestions

- Read Isaiah 61:1–3. Now, look at your own world. Where do you need to step in and start making a difference? How are you going to give beauty for ashes? Who can walk with you?
- Pray. Now get started.

N O T E S

_____

_____

_____

_____

_____

_____

_____

_____

_____

In 1845, one vote brought Texas into the Union.... In 1923, one vote gave Adolf Hitler leadership of the Nazi Party. In 1960, one vote per precinct in four states gave John F. Kennedy the presidency of the United States."

Questions and Suggestions

- Read Luke 12:6–7. How does this passage make you feel?
- When has one word or one act by one person made a huge difference in your life? When have you made that kind of difference in someone else's life?
- Pray.

Day 3
Step Out and Go

During World War II, hundreds of Bulgarian Jews had been rounded up and were gong to be sent to the Nazi concentration camp at Auschwitz. That changed when Metropolitan Kyril, a bold Christian leader in Bulgaria, walked into the barbed-wire enclosure holding the Jews. He walked past the Nazi guns into the midst of the captives and quoted Ruth 1:16. The Christians who came with Metropolitan—and the Jews—cheered. (Through the courage of Metropolitan Kyril, and others, no Bulgarian Jew ever died in a concentration camp during the War.

God's love can provide the motivation for history-changing action.

Questions and Suggestions

- Read the whole Book of Ruth for an amazing example of one person stepping out and a whole nation being transformed because of it.
- Where is one area you can "step out and go" this week? What will it take to get you to follow through? Call one person and take him or her with you.
- Pray.

Day 4
Adequate, I Think

In his book *Messy Spirituality* (Grand Rapids: Zondervan, 2002), Mike Yaconelli quoted a brief kid's letter to God:

"Dear God,
I'm doing the best I can.
Frank"

Yaconelli went on to say, "I just want to be remembered as a person who loved God, who served others more than he served himself, who was trying to grow in maturity and stability. I want to have more victories than defeats, yet here I am, almost sixty, and I fail on a regular basis" (pp 9–11).

You are one, and you matter. God doesn't ask you to have it all together before you act. He asks you to wait for him to show up, and to step out and go. That's adequate enough for God.

Questions and Suggestions

- Read Romans 5:8. How does it make you feel to know what God did for you, and the state you were in when he did it? Are you ever overwhelmed by the effort to do more or to do better?
- Be encouraged. Continue to do the best you can. Maybe that would be better said, "*Be* the best you can." God loves you.
- Pray.

Day 5
Beauty for Ashes

Have you seen the movie *Les Miserables*? The main character was having a terrible life. Jailed for trying to get food so he wouldn't starve to death, he finally got out of prison and tried to make it in life. As he moved forward, or "waited" for what was next, he was shown grace, kindness, and forgiveness—given beauty for ashes. He then devoted his

Leading into the Session

Warm Up

Option 1 Play Rock, Paper, Scissors.
LITTLE PREP *Candy or another small prize (optional)*
Option 2 Play Dodge Ball.
MORE PREP *Large, soft rubber ball(s), room to play; candy or other small prizes (optional)*

Starting Line

Option 1 Write down a revelation.
YOUNGER YOUTH *Random books, paper, pens or pencils*
Option 2 Discuss predictions.
OLDER YOUTH

Leading through the Session

Straight Away

Explore the Bible passage.
Bibles

The Turn

Talk about what God is doing.
Reproducible 1, pens or pencils; Chris Tomlin song "Famous One" (optional)

Leading beyond the Session

Home Stretch

Option 1 Define having a worldview.
YOUNGER YOUTH *Bible*
Option 2 Discuss hope.
OLDER YOUTH *Bible, Reproducible 2, pens or pencils*

Finish Line

Option 1 Thank God for his glory.
LITTLE PREP

Option 2 Fill the earth with the knowledge of God.
MORE PREP *Bibles, helium tank, balloons, pens or pencils, note cards, hole punch, yarn or ribbon*

SESSION 3

REASON TO HOPE

Bible Passage
Habakkuk 2:2–14

Key Verse
The earth will be filled with the knowledge of the glory of the LORD, as the waters cover the sea.
—Habakkuk 2:14

Main Thought
God's activity — even during tough times — is reason to hope.

Bible Background

In addition to their words of praise, the Psalms also frequently lament trouble and ask why the wicked prosper. This same theme is repeated in the opening chapter of Habakkuk. Unlike the Psalms, however, Habakkuk applied this question to the realm of international politics and their impact on the life of Judah. Interpreting the events of Israel's life against the larger backdrop of world affairs was a familiar prophetic task. So, for example, Habakkuk's older contemporary Nahum, also a prophet in the southern kingdom, celebrated the demise of the hated and feared Assyrian Empire as God's victory over wickedness. The collapse of the Assyrians was accomplished, however, at the hands of the next emerging superpower of the region, the Babylonians. The army of Judah could not match the size and weaponry of the new forces that now threatened. "The prophetic Book of Habakkuk, in the Babylonian period of Jerusalem's history, mobilizes a rich variety of extant [worship] traditions into a roughly coherent statement of faith that features *cries of need* that are ultimately resolved in a *hymn of triumph.*"[1]

The Book of Habakkuk raised the voice of Jerusalem crying in need of protection against the overwhelming force of the Babylonian aggressor. As Judah worried about the Babylonians, the residents of Jerusalem began to wonder whether God could be trusted, whether he would protect them as he had in the past. That these questions could even be posed was a sign of the deepening gloom in the capital. It is worth remembering that gloom and despair in the face of such a threat were understandable. Jerusalem was the capital of Judah and the largest city of the region, the most likely place for invaders to look for wealth and movable goods that could be taken as plunder. Moreover, ancient soldiers spared none of the peoples over whom they were victorious. Defeated warriors were put to the sword, but women and children suffered perhaps worse fates as living victims. Small wonder that Habakkuk asked why the unrighteous prospered at such cost.

Habakkuk's cry of need was matched by its strong hope in God's eventual triumph. Habakkuk 2:4 is the key to understanding the possibility of such hope and the fulcrum of the book: "the righteous will live by his faith." This faith was a trust in God even in the face of powers that threatened to overwhelm Judah. It was this verse from Habakkuk, quoted by Paul in his Roman letter (1:17), that prompted Martin Luther's evangelical insight and the spirit of his great hymn, "A Mighty Fortress Is Our God." Although the Babylonians were knocking at Jerusalem's door, bringing with them all the terrors of ancient warfare, Habakkuk called the people to move through despair to hope. They might have wanted to linger in questions that wondered about God's power or trustworthiness, but Habakkuk called them beyond that to trust in the power of a God whose righteousness would power their future and whose holiness demanded that "all the earth be silent before him" (2:20).

1. Walter Brueggemann, *An Introduction to the Old Testament: The Canon and Christian Imagination* (Louisville: Westminster John Knox Press, 2003), 240.

OPTION 1 (LITTLE PREP)

Play Rock, Paper, Scissors.

Warm Up

Conduct a tournament of Rock, Paper, Scissors. In this game, paired off players count to three together, striking one fist into the palm of the other hand on each count. At *three*, each player forms either a rock (fist), paper (flattened hand), or scissors (two fingers held out) with the fisted hand. Rock crushes scissors but is covered by paper; paper covers rock but is cut by scissors; scissors cut paper but are crushed by rock. If both students form the same item, then the round is a tie. Each pair should play for the best two out of three, then the winners should pair up and play off against one another. When you get down to the last two pairs, put them in the center of the group; everyone else should choose a contestant and cheer for him or her—the louder the better. If you wish, you can award candy or another small prize to the ultimate winner.

After you are through with the game, ask, **What is the point of Rock, Paper, Scissors?** The object is to eliminate other players by destroying their rock, paper, or scissors with *your* rock, paper, or scissors. The game is a competition, won when one person has destroyed the rocks, papers, and scissors of all other players.

Say, **Rock, Paper, Scissors is a war of sorts, with the destruction of the other players as the goal.**

. . . .

OPTION 2 (MORE PREP)

Play Dodge Ball.

Play a round or more of Dodge Ball. You can start with one half of the students around a circle throwing the ball at the other students who are in the circle, or with two equal teams throwing the ball at each other from opposing squares. Students who are hit are "out" for that round and must leave the circle or square. Be sure to find a location suitable for this activity. If you wish, you can use multiple balls to make play more interesting. You can divide the group randomly, trying to keep things even or stacking one side just for fun. You can also award candy or other small prizes to the winning individual or team.

After you are through with the game, ask, **What is the point of Dodge Ball?** The object is to eliminate players on the other team or in the center by smacking them with a ball. The game is a competition, won when one team completely destroys the other team or when no players are left in the center.

Say, **Dodge Ball is a war of sorts, with the destruction of the other team or players as the goal.**

Note:

If you sent the Portable Sanctuary home with students last week, take some time at the beginning of this session to review and discuss their experience.

Website:

For more specific rules and variations, see http://en.wikipedia.org/wiki/Dodgeball.

85

Starting Line

OPTION 1 (YOUNGER YOUTH)

Write down a revelation.

Bring to class several random books—one per student, if possible. These could be as random as a children's book, a dictionary, a college textbook, a Bible, and so forth. Give each student a book, a piece of paper, and a pen or pencil. At your word, each student should find one random fact in his or her book and write it down. After several seconds, ask students to switch books and to write down another random fact. Continue this process for a predetermined amount of time, or until every student has had every book.

Now, give each student a turn to reveal which facts he or she has written down. Did any students duplicate any facts? Who had the most unusual facts? What was revealed that no one knew before? Ask, **What is a *revelation?*** A revelation is the act of making something known, implying that the hearers did not know it before. In this activity, some revelations were made. Explain that through the writings of the prophets, God gave revelations to his people.

When you are ready to move on, say, **Let's see what God revealed through the prophet Habakkuk.**

. . . .

OPTION 2 (OLDER YOUTH)

Discuss predictions.

Go around the room and ask students to make predictions about one another. Make sure that each student has the chance to have predictions made about him or her by the other students. These predictions can be serious ("I predict that you will be a famous singer someday") or funny ("I predict that you will have twenty kids someday"), but make sure they are not hurtful or disrespectful. As the group leader, participate in making predictions, and allow students to make predictions about *your* future. After everyone has been the subject of predictions, ask, **Will any of these things come true? How can you tell?** We often make predictions based on our knowledge of a person and his or her situation. Point out that since God has perfect and complete knowledge, the things he predicts will certainly come true. Explain that through the writings of the prophets, God made predictions about his people.

When you are ready to move on, say, **Let's see what God predicted through the prophet Habakkuk.**

Explore the Bible passage.

Explain that Habakkuk had a very unique style in his prophetic writing. Most of his book is made up of questions that he posed to God, and God's answers to those questions. Really, the questions were complaints, something along the lines of, "God, why is there so much evil happening to and among your people, yet you are doing nothing about it?" The nation of Babylon was getting ready to move in and take over. The Babylonians were a violent and deadly force. Things were not looking good.

Straight Away

Read together Habakkuk 2:2–14. Discuss the following questions:

- **Why do you think God asked Habakkuk to write down the revelation that God was about to give?** When someone gives us important instructions or information, we are often asked to write it down. This is so we don't forget it, and so that we can share the information with others as needed. God told Habakkuk to write the revelation on tablets (think Moses and the Ten Commandments; paper as we know it and computers were not around back then). Invite your students to think of other ways that God might want us to share important information today: by phone, e-mail, Web site, blog, billboard, movies and music, and others.

- **What do you think verse 4 means by "wine betrays him"?** Explain that when people become drunk, they say and do things they would not say or do otherwise. This might be called "letting your guard down," or "losing your inhibitions." People under the influence of wine or other alcohol might say things they don't intend to say—criticizing others or giving away information that they shouldn't divulge. Wine "betrays" a person by letting others see what he or she is really like.

- **This passage touches on the problems of drinking, pride, greed, extortion, murder, death, and destruction. Where and how do you see these sorts of things happening in our world today?** Use wisdom with guiding the discussion here. It would be very beneficial for you to have some previous knowledge of what is happening in the world so you can share relevant and timely information. Touch on subjects such as world hunger (see www.thehungersite.com or www.worldhunger.org), the AIDS epidemic in Africa (see www.one.org), the devastation in Cambodia from the Khmer Rouge regime (see www.pepyride.org), the "invisible children" of Uganda (see www.invisiblechildren.com), slavery (see www.ijm.org), and so forth. Point out that the numbers and the weapons might have changed, but there is still pain and sorrow all over our planet.

- **Most of this passage is prophesied against the evil Babylonian invaders. How did God contrast them here with the righteous?** See verse 4. God said that the righteous live by their faith. Spend some time unpacking this concept with your students. The idea is that our pride, our possessions, our own efforts and strength are not what will ultimately sustain us; faith in God is what we need to depend on.

- **According to this passage, what will happen to Babylon (and to people who do the things that Babylon did)?** Other people will ridicule them, their debtors (those who owe them money) will band together and rebel, they will be plundered (robbed); even the stones and beams of their homes will cry out of their guilt. In other words, "what goes around comes around"—those who live like this will pay for what they have done. At some point, those who take advantage, abuse, control, put down, and hurt, will have to face the music. The very things they used to make themselves great are the very things that will be their downfall.

- **How would you paraphrase the prediction and the promise of verses 13 and 14?** No matter what the people and nations of the world do, God will have the last word. God's knowledge and glory will fill the earth.
- **What will be the timing of the fulfillment of this prediction?** This passage does not say; it just promises that God has appointed a time, and that the promise will come true when the time is right. Point out that this is a God promise, not something to be attempted by us; we simply need to live in expectation that the promise will be fulfilled.
- **What do you think it means that the earth will be filled with the knowledge of God? Don't most people already at least know who God is (even if they don't worship or serve him)?** Let students wrestle with this for a bit. This is not talking about just knowing of God or knowing who God is—it refers to "the knowledge *of the glory of the* LORD" (verse 14, emphasis added). People will see and understand that God is sovereign and active in all things, glorified by all of his creation, and worthy of our praise and devotion. The song "Come, Now Is the Time to Worship" is based on this idea: One day every tongue will confess the name of God and will bow before him; still the greatest treasure remains for those people who gladly choose to worship God now. It is the wise choice to acknowledge God's glory now instead of later!

Say, **God promised Habakkuk that God was working—even when it didn't look that way to Habakkuk.**

The Turn

Talk about what God is doing.

Distribute to students copies of "What's Going On" (Reproducible 1), go over the instructions, and allow time to complete the handout individually. If possible, play for your class the Chris Tomlin song "Famous One" and furnish or project the lyrics. When students have completed their work, call them back together and go over the questions together. Some points you may wish to consider:

- God is "famous" in the respect that he is known by many and worshiped by many.
- The intricacies of creation (cycles of nature, the planets, molecules, the complexity of the human body, and other things) could not just happen by chance—they bear witness to the great wisdom of God.
- People want God to fix their problems, to heal them, to make them rich, to make them happy, and almost every other thing that we could think of. Sometimes God does what we ask, sometimes he doesn't, and sometimes he answers in another way. Point out that when we sincerely ask for God to live in us and save us through faith in Christ, the answer is always "yes"— 100 percent of the time.

- In Habakkuk's time, God was speaking to the people and revealing what he was up to, dispensing justice and defending the oppressed, listening to the cries of the hurting, and making his glory known in the world.
- God is still speaking to people and revealing his work, helping the hurting, and making his glory known. Much of the work that God does happens through other people, or it happens so often that it is misidentified or taken for granted. Challenge your students to identify specific blessings in their lives and to consider God's involvement in these ways.

Say, **God was actively working in Habakkuk's time and he is actively doing something now, in our time—if we will just open our eyes to see it.**

Leading beyond the Session

OPTION 1 (YOUNGER YOUTH)
Define having a worldview.

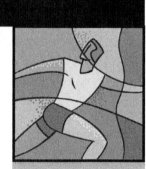

Home Stretch

Ask, **What does it mean to have a worldview? How would it be different from the usual view we have?** The short answer is pretty obvious—to have a view of the world. Invite your students to imagine being on the moon, looking back at the earth. From that perspective, we could see the whole world, not just our own area. This is exactly the concept of a worldview, but it applies to seeing the cultures, experiences, and perspectives of the other peoples of the world, not the geography! Share any or all of the following examples to help your students understand having a worldview:

- **It would look strange to us to see people driving on the left-hand side of the road—but that's how it's done in some countries.**
- **We usually expect to experience winter weather at Christmastime—but south of the equator, December 25 is in summertime.**
- **It seems natural to us to talk about and celebrate the holidays of Thanksgiving, Christmas, and Easter—but that's not done in some countries.**
- **It would be unusual for one of our church services to last four hours— but that's expected in some countries.**
- **We would say that a man having more than one wife is not normal—but it is accepted in some cultures.**

Point out that having a worldview doesn't mean we support or agree with everything done in the world; it does mean that we understand the ways that other cultures think and behave, and that we are open to dialogue with them.

Read aloud Habakkuk 2:14: **"For the earth will be filled with the knowledge of the glory of the LORD."** Explain that through a relationship with Christ, we can see and experience the glory of the Lord. The earth is already filled with God's glory in the sense that the magnificence of creation testifies to God and in the sense that there are people everywhere who know and worship God; but, there are plenty of people who still need to know God.

When you are ready to move on, say, **Some people may never get the chance to fully know the glory of the Lord, unless you and I share it with them.**

OPTION 2 (OLDER YOUTH)

Discuss hope.

Share the following quotation by reading it, distributing copies, or showing it as a projection:

"(Hope) means…a continual looking forward to the eternal world…. It does not mean that we are to leave the present world as it is. If you read history you will find that the Christians who did most for the present world were just those who thought most of the next…. It is since Christians have largely ceased to think of the other world that they have become so ineffective in this. Aim at Heaven and you will get earth 'thrown in': aim at earth and you will get neither" (C. S. Lewis, *Mere Christianity* [New York: Macmillan Publishing Company, 1952], 104).

Distribute to students copies of "Aiming at Heaven" (Reproducible 2) and allow time to complete the handout individually. After a few minutes, bring everyone back together and invite those who are willing to share their responses. Encourage students to be honest about their present and future hopes and to express things other than material needs. Read with students Ephesians 1:3–6. God wants each of us to live holy and blameless before him, and this will bring glory to God. We live in a world that is desperately in need of the knowledge of the glory of God and of the peace of God. As we live for God, we become instruments of God's work and peace in the world, spreading his glory. To "aim at heaven" means that we keep an eternal God-perspective in mind; this should affect our priorities and how we care for others. We should want to experience heaven—and to take as many people as possible there with us.

When you are ready to move on, say, **My hope for each of you is that you will live to "aim at heaven."**

Finish Line

Note:

Don't forget to distribute copies of the Portable Sanctuary to students before they go.

OPTION 1 (LITTLE PREP)

Thank God for his glory.

Allow students a time of corporate prayer focused on the things they have learned and experienced this session. Don't make everyone pray, but make sure that you give everyone the opportunity to pray. Conclude the prayer by emphasizing the reality that God is truly active and working in the world, in your community, in your church, and in the lives of your students and by thanking God for the hope we have to experience the glory of the Lord.

OPTION 2 (MORE PREP)

Fill the earth with the knowledge of God.

Provide enough helium balloons for each group member to have at least one. (You could either borrow or rent a helium tank and fill your own balloons or buy balloons that are already filled.) Furnish note cards and invite students to write the text of Habakkuk 2:14 on them. Students should then punch holes in the note cards and tie one card to each balloon. Take your balloons outside and release them together. Emphasize that God is truly active and working in the world, in your community, in your church, and in the lives of your students. Conclude the session by praying that God will work through your students to fill the whole earth with God's hope and glory.

> *Note:*
>
> Don't forget to distribute copies of the Portable Sanctuary to students before they go.

What's Going On

God was working in Habakkuk's time, and he's working now—in our time.

Would you consider God "famous" in the world? If so, how? If not, why not? _____
_____
_____

How does creation declare the greatness of God? _____
_____
_____

What do people "desire" from God? Does God provide it? Explain. _____
_____
_____

What was God doing in Habakkuk's time? _____
_____
_____

What things do you see/perceive God doing today—in your life, your family, your school, your church, your community, and the world? _____
_____
_____

Aiming at Heaven

"Aim at Heaven and you will get earth 'thrown in': aim at earth and you will get neither" (C. S. Lewis, *Mere Christianity* [New York: Macmillan Publishing Company, 1952], 104).

What things do you most hope for in life right now? _____
_____
_____
_____

What things do you most hope for in the future? _____
_____

What do you think that God hopes for in your life? _____
_____

What is your hope for this world—for God's work in this world? _____
_____

How can you be involved in seeing God's hope and God's will come to be a reality in this world? _____
_____
_____

Are you "aiming at heaven"? What does that mean? How should aiming at heaven affect the hopes we have in this life—for our own lives and for the world? _____
_____
_____

Portable Sanctuary

Day 1

Responding to the Future

In his book *A Cup of Coffee at the Soul Café* (Nashville: Broadman & Holman Publishers, 1998, 87), author Leonard Sweet quotes Eugene Peterson as saying, "Hope is a response to the future, which has its foundations in the promises of God. It looks at the future as time for the completion of God's promise.… (I)t is misunderstood if it is valued only for the comfort it brings, as if it should say, 'Everything is going to be alright in the future because God is in control of it.…' Hope operates differently. Christian hope alerts us to the possibilities of the future as a field of action, and as a consequence, fills the present with energy."

Questions and Suggestions

- Read Psalm 131. What do you think it means to "respond to the future"? How are you responding to the future? Is your response taking you to a place of involvement in the world around you (a place of action)? How?
- The future has great possibilities—what are some of your possibilities?
- Pray.

Day 2

The Orange Stripe

When I was in high school, I really wanted a car. So I found one I liked and brought my mom along "for the ride." I tried to convince her that I *really* needed this 1987 Toyota truck. It was still at the dealership, white with an orange stripe. I was hoping I would receive this truck as

Questions and Suggestions

- Read Habakkuk 2:2–14 again. How is your life different today than it was five days ago? How is God working? How is the glory of the Lord being shown?
- Enjoy exploring. Pursue incredible dreams. Discover more than what you were looking for.
- Pray.

N O T E S

_____

_____

_____

_____

_____

_____

_____

_____

_____

_____

_____

_____

_____

_____

_____

a gift—sooner than later. I talked all about how great it was and how great I would be driving it, and I appealed to my mom's sense of color when I told her the orange stripe matched my hair color, kind of. Well, my hopes for that particular truck were dashed on the rocks. I never saw that truck again—yet I still love my mom, and I have driven many other cars.

Questions and Suggestions

• Read Psalm 25:1–7. Rewrite it in your own words. Do you want God to guide you in truth? Why is your hope in him?

• Mercy is undeserved love, grace, and forgiveness. Are you a person who shows mercy? Do others see it? Do you share the mercy you have received from others? What is God revealing to you this week?

• Pray.

Day 3
Anxiously Waiting

In the Sept/Oct 2006 issue of *Relevant Magazine*, worship leader David Crowder wrote, "I want to live a faith that is a reflection of the cost of its eternal origin, not merely a reflection of my transient one. I want to feel the reality of where we sit. That the things we decide here are eternal ones. That our conversations mean something. I want to live in a manner that feels heroic, that turns the invisible into the visible, that is a solid intrusion of the eternal into the divided streets of humanity."

Questions and Suggestions

• Read Psalm 33:20–22. What do you wait for? Is your hope placed in material possessions, or is it invested in eternal things?

• How can you be God's hero, allowing him to work through you to touch others' lives in real and tangible ways? What do you hope God will do with your life?

• Pray.

Day 4
What Are You Certain Of?

Sometimes a mistake can bring something good into our lives. In 1886, a pharmacist named John Pemberton cooked up a new medicinal syrup. He figured this would be a great remedy for people who were tired, nervous, or plagued with sore teeth. When the assistant made up the next batch, he accidentally used carbonated water in the mix. Instead of medicine, these men ended up with a fizzy beverage—one that is now consumed around the world. Each day, over 1 billion Coca-Cola drinks are guzzled on this planet.

Questions and Suggestions

• Read Hebrews 11 (the whole chapter). Our deepest hope is often to never make a mistake or to always be safe. What did these people hope for (what did they place their faith in)?

• How should our hope lead us? Should it put our focus on safety or take us out into the open world of possibilities? Why? Is your hope changing? How?

• Pray.

Day 5
How's Your Hope?

Mark Twain once said, "Twenty years from now you will be more disappointed by the things that you didn't do than by the ones you did do. So throw off the bowlines. Sail away from the safe harbor. Catch the trade winds in your sails. Explore. Dream. Discover." We hope this week has brought you some challenges, some opportunities to look beyond the end of whatever is happening now, and the ability to say, "Okay, God, let's hit this great adventure at full speed."

Leading into the Session

Warm Up

Option 1 *Little Prep* Compare the church to a football game.

Option 2 *More Prep* Take and discuss a group photo.
Equipment to take and display a picture

Starting Line

Option 1 *Younger Youth* Go look at your name.

Option 2 *Older Youth* Google your name.
Reproducible 1, pens or pencils, computer and Internet access (during or before class time)

Leading through the Session

Straight Away

Explore the Bible passage.
Bibles, chalkboard or dry erase board

The Turn

Discuss losing the house.
Bibles, Reproducible 2, pens or pencils

Leading beyond the Session

Home Stretch

Option 1 *Younger Youth* Go on a drive.
Information for conducting a toy drive or other collection effort

Option 2 *Older Youth* Look at what you want to be.
Butcher paper, colored markers

Finish Line

Option 1 *Little Prep* Proclaim the word of the Lord at the gate.

Option 2 *More Prep* Go to a forsaken place.
Visit to an abandoned church, building, or neighborhood

WHAT GOES AROUND, COMES AROUND

Bible Passage
Jeremiah 7:1–15

Key Verses
If you really change your ways and your actions . . . then I will let you live in this place . . . for ever and ever.
—Jeremiah 7:5, 7

Main Thought
God helps us to know and do what he asks.

As early as 626 BC or perhaps as late as 609 BC the prophet Jeremiah began delivering his unique message of judgment followed by comfort to the city of Jerusalem. More than any other of the prophets of Israel, Jeremiah's ministry strode across the Babylonian crisis from just prior to the acute point of attack in 587 BC through deportations and, finally, exile. He delivered this message from the perspective of an outsider, a religious figure—indeed a priest, but one who came to Jerusalem from the village of Anatoth in the region of the tribe of Benjamin. That district lay in the shattered remains of the northern kingdom that had been devastated a century earlier by the Assyrians. In this respect Jeremiah was quite different from the well-connected Jerusalem insider Isaiah. Although both men warned Judah of God's coming judgment, their very different origins and angles of vision illustrate the great variety to be found among the prophets.

Jeremiah began preaching during Jerusalem's worst period of religious and moral decay. The word of the Lord came to him during the reign of King Amon, whose fate was to be murdered in a palace revolt on account of his continuation of the disastrous policies of the wicked Manasseh. Today's passage clearly describes Jerusalem's debased religious climate. The worship of Baal had been introduced and in the very temple of God his people were following practices that Jeremiah labeled "detestable." Jeremiah indicted Jerusalem for its disobedience to the commandments of God found in Torah. He followed up this indictment with a sentence of punishment—Jerusalem and Judah would suffer destruction and a Babylonian assault that they should understand to be the will of God.

Obedience to Torah as the proper means by which Israel was to keep its covenant with God was still a fairly recent ideal in Jeremiah's time. This view was basic to the Book of Deuteronomy and the so-called "Deuteronomistic theology."

However, as documented in 2 Kings 22 and 23, Deuteronomy was only discovered in the temple during the reign of the boy king Josiah, a discovery dated to 621 BC, and very possibly within Jeremiah's early ministry. Fundamental to Deuteronomy was the idea that God blesses the righteous and punishes the wicked, and that Torah obedience was the standard by which righteousness and wickedness were to be measured. To keep covenant with God meant to keep God's Torah. But other voices could be heard in Jerusalem advocating different interpretations of covenant obedience. Embedded in the priestly class was a point of view that asserted that proper worship constituted covenant loyalty. Still others took the extreme position that God had made an absolute covenant with Israel through David—obedience was not an issue and Jerusalem need not fear the Babylonians because David's dynasty would rule there forever. Against priests and advocates of a royal ideology Jeremiah spoke a message that tied Israel's covenant to obedience to Torah. Jeremiah 7:3–15 makes explicitly clear the depths of Jerusalem's disobedience and the extent of the punishment about to be inflicted. All the people had to do was turn their eyes to the north and remember the sad fate of the northern kingdom of Israel, also called Ephraim, for a preview of the events about to unfold in their own midst.

OPTION 1 (LITTLE PREP)

Compare the church to a football game.

Say, **The church has been compared to a football game—22,000 people who are badly in need of exercise watching twenty-two people who are badly in need of rest play the game.** Invite students to discuss what they think this statement means. Many churches operate like football, as "spectator sports"; the few staff members or leaders "perform" or do the work, and everyone else sits in the pew and watches. Say, **Imagine our own congregation or youth group as a football game. Where do you see yourself in the picture? Are you on the field playing the game? If so, which player are you? Are you coaching? Are you a referee? Are you a cheerleader? Are you a spectator in the stands? Are you usually just an empty seat?** The goal is not to imply specific responses to this question but instead to help students begin thinking about God's will for his people.

Say, **God calls us to be on his team—and to be engaged in the game.**

Warm Up

Note:

If you sent the Portable Sanctuary home with students last week, take some time at the beginning of this session to review and discuss their experience.

• •

OPTION 2 (MORE PREP)

Take and discuss a group photo.

Take a group photo of your students and display it for them to see. You might also have it blown up to poster size (this can be done at many copy centers), label and date it, and post it in your meeting room. If possible, you coul make copies on the spot and distribute them to your students. You could also e-mail the picture or instantly project it for the whole class to see. After you have taken the picture, ask, **What has changed since this picture was taken? What will change about this group over the next year?** Invite students to respond. Each of you has already aged a few seconds or minutes, and you could never duplicate the exact pose again. Chances are, your group will be significantly different in a year—some current people will be gone and some new faces present, and some tragedies or other substantial events may alter the lives of group members. Point out that a picture is a snapshot in time, showing what things used to be like at a particular instant.

Say, **Pictures help us to see how things have changed over time.**

OPTION 1 (YOUNGER YOUTH)

Go look at your name.

Take your students outside of your meeting place to look at the sign that identifies your location. If you're at a church building or rented facility, this would be the sign out front; if you meet in someone's home, look for the family's name on the front of the house or mailbox, or an address. Ask, **What does this sign tell us?** The sign indicates the name of the facility, the group that uses the facility, or the family who lives there. An address sign indicates a unique and specific location, which helps to identify the associated facility, group, or family. Point out that when

Starting Line

you see the name on a particular sign, you know what to expect when you go inside.

When you are ready to move on, say, **Let's see what God had to say about the people on his team, the people who shared his name—what they used to do, and how they had changed.**

. . . .

OPTION 2 (OLDER YOUTH)

Google your name.

If you have computer and Internet access during class time, let your students use a search engine such as Google to find their names on the Web. If you can't be on the Web during class time, you can research students' names beforehand, print out the results, and bring them with you. (**Hint:** Use quotes around the names so that you get more specific results.) Provide copies of "What's in a Name?" (Reproducible 1) for students to use to take notes about what they find. Who else in the world shares your students' names? What do those people do? Ask, **What does your name—or any person's name—indicate?** Names themselves have root meanings; more specifically, they are used to identify each of us as unique among people. A name is used to identify who you are. Point out that when you hear the name of a person you know, you know what to expect.

When you are ready to move on, say, **Let's see what God had to say about the people on his team, the people who shared his name—what they used to do, and how they had changed.**

Note:

Be careful not to navigate to any Websites with objectionable content.

Straight Away

Leading through the Session

Explore the Bible passage.

Share with your students any information from the Bible Background that you feel will help them understand Jeremiah's perspective and situation. Jeremiah was young when he became a prophet, perhaps a teenager. He prophesied during the reign of several kings and leaders. God had Jeremiah do some creative and unusual things to get the people's attention and get the message across: shouting out in public; using a belt as an object lesson, breaking a clay jar, and buying a field. God even told him not to get married because things were going to get so bad in the country! Jeremiah spent a lot of time in prison, and was threatened several times because he spoke the truth and others were not willing to hear it. However, even when faced with the threat of losing his own life, Jeremiah faithfully followed the instructions of God.

Read together Jeremiah 7:1–15. Discuss the following questions:

- **Jeremiah spoke his message at the gate of the Lord's house. Some scholars think that this was during one of the three annual feasts when all the men of the area were to appear before God. Basically, Jeremiah went to the place where everyone would be. How would people react if someone stood at the front of our church before worship and was criticizing the church? Where might someone stand today if he or she** wanted to get a message to "everybody"? Someone "causing trouble" before church services would probably be encouraged to stop—nicely at first, then more forcefully. Ask students to think of the places in your community where the largest crowds gather. Outside a movie theater or a shopping mall might be the place where Jeremiah would preach today.

- **Jeremiah told the people to reform (change) their ways. What were the things they needed to change?** Write responses on the board. Jeremiah mentioned deceptive words (lies); injustice; oppression of aliens (foreigners), orphans, and widows; shedding innocent blood (murder); following other gods (placing other things before God); stealing; and adultery. Point out that God repeatedly expressed that he did not approve of these things—yet the people kept doing them.

- **What were the people trying to do by repeating, "This is the temple of the LORD" three times?** They felt they could get *away* with whatever they wanted as long as they "went to church." The repetition of the phrase is sort of like saying a magic formula to make everything better. The people thought they could keep God in their back pocket like a "get out of hell free" card. But God was done with this kind of living.

- **Look at the list we have just made. Does this kind of stuff happen in the church today?** Encourage students to take a real look at the way people live *away* from church/youth group and how they act *at* church/youth group. Some people live completely contrary to God's Word all week and then show up for church and act like perfect Christians. Some people "follow other gods" by compromising to get popularity or to look/dress right. Chances are that you have students who come from broken homes, whose parents have been involved in adultery, and who are themselves sexually active? The idea here is to pursue God's will when we know it, not to feel bad about past mistakes or about what we did *before* we knew God. God does have standards, and God does ask us to keep them.

- **God indicated that his people were not living up to his name. Are there any things about our church or group that do not fit well with a place that carries the Name of God?** Invite students to respond. Do not let this become a gripe session where students put down the church. Rather, let it be an exercise in opening eyes to what really matters about the people who gather in God's name. Be constructive.

- **Jeremiah told the people that God had been watching them. God *still* watches. God watches us. What does that say about God? How does the fact that God is watching make you feel?** God cares about who we are and what we do; God is active and involved, participating in our lives. God desires the best for us. There is comfort in this—and encouragement to do right.

- **Jeremiah referred to Shiloh (verses 12–15), the place where the ark of the Covenant used to stay. But the people disobeyed God, were defeated by the Philistines, and the ark was captured (see 1 Samuel 4). What does the fact that the ark didn't protect Israel from the enemy suggest?** Simply "playing the Christian game" or going through the motions when there is no real evidence of following God in our lives does nothing for us. It's false religion, and it's worthless.

- **Someone might read this and think that God is sitting in heaven with a "holy fly-swatter," waiting to smash us if we blow it. How would you respond to that?** The Bible makes clear God's great love for us; this passage makes clear that God warns us and pleads with us when we are in jeopardy. God makes it clear what he expects—and he is actively involved in helping us to do what he asks.

Say, **Through Jeremiah, God helped the people to know and do what he asked.**

The Turn

Discuss losing the house.

Distribute to students copies of "Snapshots" (Reproducible 2), or show it as a projection. You can either work through this exercise together or allow students to work on it in small groups and then bring everyone back together to share their responses. For the sake of time, you can assign the different passages to different groups or group members. Suggested answers are as follows:

- Genesis 12:1–3—God spoke to Abraham and promised to bless him and all the peoples on earth through him. This was a high point.
- Exodus 14:10–31—God miraculously parted the Red Sea and freed the Israelites from slavery in Egypt. This was a high point.
- Numbers 14:1–12—God brought the people to the Promised Land, but they were scared to go in. This was a low point.
- 1 Samuel 17:1–11, 38–50—God miraculously delivered the Israelites from Goliath and the Philistines through David. This was a high point.
- 1 Kings 8:62–66—The temple was dedicated, and Solomon made huge sacrifices in God's honor. This was a high point.
- 2 Kings 16:1–4—The king of Judah sacrificed his own son in the fire as an offering to other gods. This was a low point.
- 2 Kings 25:1–7—God's city, Jerusalem, was captured and destroyed by the Babylonians. This was a low point.

Point out that God did some huge things for the Israelites, but the passion of the people for God never lasted long. The Israelites finally "lost the house"—their nation was dismantled and destroyed. We see this same pattern today. After the terrorist attacks of September 11, 2001, churches in the United States were full—for a few months. Even on a yearly basis, many churches are full—on Easter. Looking at these "snapshots" of people's faith should tell us that how we live matters more than going to church, and who we are is more important than looking good and making a good impression on others.

Say, **Snapshots of *our* lives should show that we are staying true to the Word of God.**

OPTION 1 (YOUNGER YOUTH)

Go on a drive.

Before class, find a local charity to which you can donate toys or other collected items. Make plans with your students to conduct a toy drive or similar collection effort for this organization. Work together to set dates, times, and goals. If this idea works out, you may consider making it an annual effort for your group. You might also get other members of the church or community involved in your efforts. Help your students to realize that their lives and their efforts matter—especially in a world that so desperately needs God's healing activity.

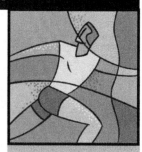

Home Stretch

When you are ready to move on, say, **When we act with compassion toward others, we show that we understand what God asks.**

• •

OPTION 2 (OLDER YOUTH)

Look at what you want to be.

Bring to class a good supply of butcher paper and colored markers, and invite students to trace their own outlines. If you have limited paper or a large group, they can trace heads only; for smaller groups, they can trace their entire bodies. Ask students to write their names on their outlines and to add some distinguishing characteristics (hair, eyes, and so forth) that will help to identify them. You can either post the outlines on the wall or leave them on the floor or table. When the outlines are complete, ask students to write two things on their own outlines:

1. How God has blessed them.
2. How they are (and can be) a blessing to others.

Next, have each student go to the other students' outlines and write the following:

1. How God has blessed this person.
2. How this person is (and can be) a blessing to others.

When this is done, allow time for students to read their own outlines. Did they learn anything about how others see God's work in their lives? If so, what?

When you are ready to move on, say, **Through your actions, you can show that God is truly working in your life.**

Finish Line

Note:

Don't forget to distribute copies of the Portable Sanctuary to students before they go.

OPTION 1 (LITTLE PREP)

Proclaim the word of the Lord at the gate.

Pray over your students, asking God to help them grow in grace and in the knowledge of his Word. Then, conclude your session by going to the "gate" and proclaiming the word of the Lord: Go to the sanctuary entrance of your church or other location where the most people come in. As the people enter, your students should offer words of blessing from the Lord—phrases such as "God bless you!" or "Welcome! God loves you!" or "God welcomes you to enjoy his presence today!" Encourage your students that they are following in the tradition of the prophets whenever they proclaim God's Word.

OPTION 2 (MORE PREP)

Go to a forsaken place.

Make arrangements for your group to visit a forsaken, abandoned, or run-down building in your town. *(Note:* Be sure you have the proper permission to take your group off-site, and beware of trespassing violations or dangerous buildings.) If possible, do some research to find out what used to occupy the space and what happened to that organization over time. Perhaps there is a church building where the congregation declined and finally disbanded, a factory where the business went bankrupt, or a house where the people just never kept it up and it finally became unrepairable. Ask, **What happened to this place? Why is it forsaken?** Find out what students know, and share what you know. Explain that to be *forsaken* means to be abandoned, that people have left and given up on a place (or even a person). Encourage your students not to forsake God and their faith, as the people in Jeremiah's time did.

Pray for your group, asking God to continually help the students know and do what he asks.

What's in a Name?

What Websites have your name?

_____
_____
_____
_____

Which sites actually refer to you?

_____
_____
_____
_____

Who else in the world shares your name?

_____
_____
_____
_____

Snapshots

Instructions: Look up the Scripture passages that go with each picture below. Write down the details for each passage, and indicate whether you think this was a high point or a low point in the life of the people of God.

Genesis 12:1–3

Exodus 14:10–31

Numbers 14:1–12

1 Samuel 17:1–11, 38–50

1 Kings 8:62–66

2 Kings 16:1–4

2 Kings 25:1–7

Portable Sanctuary

spoke to this in Deuteronomy 30. First, he said all that the people needed to know to move forward and seize their divine moment was right in front of them. Then God pointed to two paths: one leading to life and the other to death. God urged the people to choose life. He asks us to do the same.

Questions and Suggestions

• Read Deuteronomy 30 (the entire chapter). How are *you* choosing life?

• What things has God set before you to guide you along your life's journey?

• Pray.

N O T E S

Day 1
Steak or Hot Dogs?

The Apostle Peter had some advice for us as followers of Christ: "You, friends, are well-warned. Be on your guard lest you lose your footing and get swept off your feet by...lawless and loose-talking teachers. Grow in grace and understanding of our Master and Savior, Jesus Christ" (2 Peter 3:17–18, *The Message*). Singer/songwriter Ben Kweller talked about growth this way: "When you're a teenager, you know how to make some really good nachos, but as an adult you might know how to grill a filet mignon perfectly" ("All Grown Up," *Relevant Magazine*, Issue 23, Nov–Dec 2006, p 59).

Questions and Suggestions

• If you're already "well-warned" about something, it means you know what's going on—you know the dangers. What do you know about Jesus? What are the dangers of walking away from the will of God? How would that impact your life?

• What are you learning lately about the Lord? Are there some things you can do today to help you grow in grace and understanding of our Lord and Savior Jesus Christ? Spiritually speaking, are you still making nachos, or have you moved on to filet mignon?

• Pray.

Day 2
Source of Life

An acorn is the source of an oak tree. First, it has to fall to the ground and die. But out of that death comes the beginning of life—an amazing and abundant life. Oak trees are huge, and their wood is very strong. From the death of an acorn comes a place that many creatures call home—shade, food, oxygen, nutrients for the soil, and even other oak trees. All the oak tree has to do is be itself, and life springs forth. If we are in Christ, we can be ourselves—our *new* selves. Jesus will bring forth life through us.

Questions and Suggestions

• Read John 10:7-18. Look at the world around you. Do you recognize the thieves? How can you tell the difference?
• How is your life different now than when you first started following Christ? Are you living more abundantly? Is the life of Christ flowing through you?
• Pray.

Day 3
Saving Grace

I read this once on the BBC Sports Web site: "England's victory was made possible by a superlative knock from Trescothick, who made a 60-ball 82 with 11 fours a 66-run seventh wicket partnership between Stewart and Collingwood, both of whom scored 38 with Stewart remaining unbeaten." I don't even begin to remotely understand what that means. But I do understand this in the Bible: "Is it not clear to you that to go back to that old rule-keeping, peer-pleasing religion would be an abandonment of everything personal and free in my relationship with God? I refuse to do that, to repudiate God's grace. If a living relationship with God could come by rulekeeping, then Christ died unnecessarily" (Galatians 2:20–21, *The Message*).

I am so glad that I am not expected to fit into a little box. I love the fact that grace and a living relationship with God are given freely.

• Pray.

Questions and Suggestions

• Take a few moments to think about God's grace in your life and to write about it. How do you see it? How can you recognize it working from day to day?
• How are you living as an example of free grace and a life-giving relationship with God?
• Pray.

Day 4
Maintaining Momentum

In the book *The City of God* (New York: Random House, 1993, 867), Fifth-century Christian philosopher Augustine described heaven like this: "There we shall rest and see, see and love, love and praise. This is what shall be in the end without end. For what other end do we propose to ourselves than to attain to the kingdom of which there is no end?" The Apostle Paul put it this way: "When perfection comes, the imperfect disappears.... Now we see but a poor reflection as in a mirror; then we shall see face to face. Now I know in part; then I shall know fully, even as I am fully known" (1 Corinthians 13:10, 12).

Questions and Suggestions

• Read 1 Corinthians 13 (the entire chapter). What is so perfect about love? How is love a sign of true spiritual maturity?
• How does looking to eternity touch the way you live now? Where are you doing well? What life adjustments should you make?
• Pray.

Day 5
Now Choose Life

Remember the Garden of Eden? Everything was perfect, until one poor choice was made. How could they mess up when they had everything going their way? How frustrating. Now it seems as if we are surrounded by endless wrong choices as we search for the elusive right one. God

Leading into the Session

Warm Up

Option 1
LITTLE PREP
Make plans for your students.
Digital BRIDGES CD, computer, and printer prior to class time (optional)

Option 2
MORE PREP
Watch a television show.
Episode of the Andy Griffith Show and the necessary equipment to watch it

Starting Line

Option 1
YOUNGER YOUTH
Play "Carnac the Magnificent."
Envelopes, turban or robe or other costume

Option 2
OLDER YOUTH
Discuss: Who are "prophets and diviners" today?
Chalkboard or dry erase board

Leading through the Session

Straight Away

Explore the Bible passage.
Bibles

The Turn

Look closer at God's plans.
Bibles

Leading beyond the Session

Home Stretch

Option 1
YOUNGER YOUTH
Practice a "forced exile."

Option 2
OLDER YOUTH
Discuss what happens in exile.
Chalkboard or dry erase board

Finish Line

Option 1
LITTLE PREP
Give thanks for what you have.
Reproducible 2

Option 2
MORE PREP
Grow where you're planted.
Seeds for tomatoes, squash, or other plants; place and time to plant and tend the seeds

---

SESSION 5

PLANS FOR PROSPERITY

Bible Passage
Jeremiah 29:4–14

Key Verse
"For I know the plans I have for you," declares the LORD, "plans to prosper you and not to harm you, plans to give you hope and a future."
—Jeremiah 29:11

Main Thought
God's plan—his will for us—is to give us hope and a future.

In the opening verses of the Book of Jeremiah we read of the prophet's call by God. God said to the prophet-to-be, "See, today I appoint you over nations and kingdoms to uproot and tear down, to destroy and overthrow, to build and to plant" (1:10). These six verbs define in summary fashion the content of Jeremiah's message. In 587 BC the army of Nebuchadnezzar, King of Babylon, brought home to Jerusalem all the terror and dismay of the first four verbs. The monarchy of Judah—the line of David—was overthrown and the city destroyed. The temple and city walls were pulled down and the lives of thousands of men, women, and children were uprooted as they were marched off to exile in a foreign land hundreds of miles from home. This exile was accomplished in a series of deportations that actually began before the destruction of Jerusalem. It was only after the leadership proved unwilling to live under Babylonian authority that Nebuchadnezzar ordered an all-out invasion. Inevitably, plundering and destruction followed, until the last of the population was deported.

Jeremiah lived through the destruction, but he was not among those selected for transport to Babylon. A shred of the city's population was left behind to sit in the rubble and figure out a way to eke out a living. Some of this remainder abandoned the city for a colony of Jewish people living at Elephantine in Egypt. There is some belief that Jeremiah may eventually have joined them. But before the close of his life and ministry there remained the fulfillment of the last two verbs in 1:10—to build and to plant. In addition to the four verbs of destruction, these two hopeful verbs were also elements of Jeremiah's preaching. He has traditionally been called the "weeping prophet," but his message embraced more than destruction and tears. The text of his letter to the exiles embedded in Jeremiah 29 offered words of hope to a people filled with grief and despair and tempted to listen to voices that would turn those emotions into rage and revolt.

It is important to note that Jeremiah was not the only person interpreting Jerusalem's situation during the Babylonian crisis. There was, as a counter example, the court prophet Hananiah who counseled resistance to all foreign aggressors. He could not accept Jeremiah's view that the Babylonians were the instrument of God intended to punish Jerusalem and Judah for their sin. Hananiah's policy of resistance may have been based on misplaced confidence in the royal ideology that David's descendants would never lose the throne. Jeremiah's letter makes reference to "prophets and diviners" among the exiles who seem to have counseled resistance to their captors, perhaps in the tradition of the royal ideology. Against such counsel Jeremiah used the two verbs "build" and "plant." In so doing he tried to teach the people to accept their exile for what it was—God's punishment. Jeremiah understood God's intention: through this punishment the exiles would be cleansed and ultimately renewed. Building and planting in Babylon were the first steps in that renewal and thus preliminary to a later building and planting that would take place back in Judah after the exile was over and God had taken his people home.

OPTION 1 (LITTLE PREP)

Make plans for your students.

Prior to class, make up some different obscure, off-the-wall plans for each of your students. For example, you might write, *James will someday discover oil in his backyard, become a billionaire, and then donate all the money to the policeman's retirement fund.* Have some fun with issues or ideas that relate personally to your students. If you think you might have some guests present, make up a few generic plans and have them ready. If you have access to the Digital BRIDGES CD, a computer, and a printer before class time, you can customize and print out the form that is found there. In class, read each student's plans aloud. After you have read them all, ask, **Do you think these things will really come true?** Perhaps not, in most of the cases; it depends on how "far out" you were, and how many personal facts you used to make your plans.

Say, **Even though these plans were just for fun, there are real plans for your life. Your parents make them, you make them, and God makes them.**

Note:

If you sent the Portable Sanctuary home with students last week, take some time at the beginning of this session to review and discuss their experience.

OPTION 2 (MORE PREP)

Watch a television show.

Bring to class an episode of the *Andy Griffith Show* and the necessary equipment to watch it. The episode you select should be one that shows Otis or other people locked up in one of Mayberry's jail cells. The idea is to show how "posh" those jail cells were—furniture, lamps, fancy bedding—and the fact that the cell door key was always hanging just outside the cell door! Just a minute or two of the episode will do. Otis appears in many episodes of the show, but following are some that center on his character (the episode numbers are continuous from the first season):

- Season 1, Episode 25—"A Plaque for Mayberry"
- Season 2, Episode 55—"Aunt Bee the Warden"
- Season 2, Episode 63—"Deputy Otis"
- Season 4, Episode 114—"Hot Rod Otis"
- Season 5, Episode 142—"Otis Sues the County"
- Season 5, Episode 145—"The Rehabilitation of Otis"
- Season 6, Episode 175—"Otis the Artist"
- Season 7, Episode 202—"Otis the Deputy"

Ask, **Why would Otis "make himself comfortable" in a jail cell? Why would the police department make him comfortable there?** Otis knew he was going to end up in the jail cell most every night—and so did the police department. Everyone decided to just make the best of the situation.

Say, **It's possible—and sometimes it's good—to make the best out of a bad situation.**

Website:

For more information on the *Andy Griffith Show,* see www. imayberry.com and http:// en.wikipedia. org/wiki/ The_Andy_ Griffith_Show.

Starting Line

Note:

For added effect, you may wish to recruit a guest to come in and play Carnac.

OPTION 1 (YOUNGER YOUTH)

Play "Carnac the Magnificent."

(*Note:* If you are unfamiliar with Johnny Carson's "Carnac the Magnificent" skits from the old Tonight Show episodes, see http://en.wikipedia.org/wiki/ Carnac_the_Magnificent. If you can wear an elaborate turban and robe or other costume, that will add to the effect.)

Prior to class, cut apart "Carnac's Clues" (Reproducible 1) and seal each one in an individual, numbered envelope. Announce to your students that you are "Carnac the Magnificent" and that the questions in the envelopes you hold were hermetically sealed and have been kept in a mayonnaise jar on Bill Gates' porch since noon yesterday. Say, **With my amazing powers I will now predict the answers to these questions, one at a time.** Hold one envelope up to your head, announce the "answer" to the question inside, and then open the envelope and read the question. Do this for each of the envelopes. Unless you can memorize the answers, you will need to have them stashed somewhere, written on your palm, or something similar.

After you have finished with all the envelopes, ask, **How many of you think that I really have the ability to predict things in this way?** No one will think so. Point out that the whole point of these skits was to ridicule such an idea.

When you are ready to move on, say, **Let's see what God—the planner of our futures—has to say about what's coming.**

· ·

OPTION 2 (OLDER YOUTH)

Discuss: Who are "prophets and diviners" today?

Explain that in the time of the Old Testament, God frequently spoke to the people through "prophets" or "diviners"—men and women who sensed or heard a message from God and then shared that message with the rest of the nation. Ask, **Who are the "prophets and diviners" in our world today—the people who claim the authority to comment on our society and to state how things should change?** Write students' responses on the board. In North American culture, this role is assigned to politicians with increasing frequency. We expect those in elected office to be sensitive to the will of the people, but we also expect them to set direction and cast vision, to state where the country needs to be headed and to implement the steps necessary to take us there. Preachers and people within the church seem to have less and less clout when speaking to those outside the church. Within the religious spectrum, leaders in some groups make frequent and specific predictions about the future. With the variety of churches to choose from in most towns and with the increasing willingness of many Christians to "church shop" outside their own denomination or church group, a lot of people won't put up with a "prophet" or "diviner" who says or does things they don't like; they simply go to a different church where they like what is being said. Point out that having variety is good, but we must be careful in our efforts to discern true "prophets and diviners" without avoiding or discarding the truth.

When you are ready to move on, say, **Let's see what Jeremiah had to say about true "prophets and diviners" in his time.**

112

Explore the Bible passage.

Read together Jeremiah 29:4–14. Discuss the following questions:

Straight Away

- **How would you interpret God's instructions in verses 4–6? Does God expect everyone to be a farmer and to have lots of kids?** To the people of Jeremiah's time, these were the normal, everyday things of life; this was saying, "Carry on as usual." It would be like God telling your students, "I know things are rough right now, but eat your Taco Bell meal, study your math and history, and go out with your buddies on Friday night."

- **God's people were in exile. They had been forcibly removed from their own homes and were living against their will in a foreign land. Why would God tell them to settle down and "conduct life as normal" in this place?** God is the one who sent them into exile (v 7). God knew that the people's time in exile was limited (v 10). God promised to prosper and bless his people—even in tough times such as exile.

- **In recent history, when have there been people groups who had to make the best of life, even when they were stuck far away from home?** Jewish people have done this for many years and many have continued to do so, even after the modern nation of Israel was established in 1948 (by 2005, there were more Jews living in the United States than in Israel). In North America, there are large groups of Hmong people who fled Laos after the Vietnam War. Many people from Iraq have fled their homes and are living in exile today because of the dangerous living conditions in Iraq.

- **How does your success in life depend on the success of your city, your school, your family, or any other larger group that you are invested in?** Invite students to respond. If a city is having economic troubles, it can cause stores to close, real estate values to go down, other companies to close, and your parents to lose their jobs. A school that is having troubles can fail to attract good teachers, which means the students don't learn as much, which affects their grades and their potential to be accepted by good colleges. Many of your students will probably be aware that a troubled family affects the student's grades, social life, and whole outlook on life. This is a principle that applies in all of life, not just in the Christian community: When the group you are a part of does well, you tend to do well too—and vice-versa.

- **Why would some prophets say the wrong thing to God's people, even though they should have known better? How do we deal with "conflicting signals" from different leaders? Whom do we believe?** Sometimes people just get the wrong message; sometimes they knowingly choose the wrong message because it makes things better for them, or because they don't want to believe that things are as bad as they really are. If all else seems equal and there's no other evidence, then time will show who was right. Time would prove that Jeremiah was telling the truth, when the people were allowed to return to Jerusalem later just as Jeremiah had said.

- **What did God promise near the end of this passage? How did that fit in with where the people were at that point in time?** God promised to bring the people back home, to give them hope and a future, and to bless them.

113

However, this would not occur until a couple of generations had passed from the scene (just as we could expect our grandparents and parents to be gone in seventy or so years). Emphasize that God was still blessing the people as they waited in exile, and that it often takes time for the "big picture" of God's plans to come to pass.

- **In what areas of your life are you in "exile"? How could you make the best of those situations by seeking peace and prosperity?** Invite students to respond. Perhaps some of your class members have moved with their families and find themselves in towns and schools that are "foreign" and unfamiliar. Sometimes changes with our existing friends can place us in "exile," even though we have not moved. Encourage students to share openly, and encourage them that God does bless us during and beyond the times of exile.
- **Lots of people attend church or claim in other ways to be "seeking God." According to this passage, what is the key to really finding God?** See verse 13. Our seeking must be *wholehearted.* Encourage students to help you define this concept; it refers to a sincere, honest seeking—not for show, but because someone really wants to find God. Point out that even people in church will not find God if they are not wholeheartedly seeking him; and, people who have never darkened the doorway of a church can still find God when they are wholeheartedly seeking him.

Say, **God had plans for his people—plans to give them hope and a future.**

The Turn

Look closer at God's plans.

Read again Jeremiah 29:11. Say, **This verse promises that God wants to prosper us, not harm us, and give us hope and a future. What do people expect God to do for them based on this verse? What does this verse mean to you personally?** Invite students to respond. The word *prosper* brings up images of money and wealth to many people. Some Christians teach that it is God's desire for each of us to have a lot of money. Help your students understand that there is a lot more to prospering than money; in fact, *prosper* often has less to do with money and more to do with relationships, peace, and the flow of life from day to day. God's people have often struggled with why the wicked seem to prosper, while the righteous seem to suffer (see Psalm 73 and Luke 13:1–5). Ask, **How do you think God wants to prosper your life? What kind of hope and future does God want to give you?** Perhaps God wants to bless your students with rich relationships, with the chance to be used for his glory, with a future full of God working through their lives. Share your own ideas and feelings about God's plans for you personally. Encourage your students to take the promise of Jeremiah 29:11 to heart and to rejoice in the power and potential of this promise.

Say, **God has plans for you personally—plans to give you hope and a future.**

114

OPTION 1 (YOUNGER YOUTH)

Practice a "forced exile."

Help your students to understand (in a small way!) the experience and feelings of being in exile by placing them in a situation where they are not familiar or comfortable. Perhaps you can ask (not force) a couple to make a speech or sing an impromptu solo in front of your group; maybe you can take the whole group to an adult class and ask (not force) them to talk or share in front of the adults; if you have a larger group, you can simulate the separation aspect of exile by purposely pairing students off with people they do not know well and asking them to pray or share in those pairs. The idea is to move students out of their usual surroundings and away from their usual buddies. After your exile is through, invite students to reflect on their experiences. Explain that you have simulated, in small fashion, the experience the Israelites of Jeremiah's day went through: they lost their families, their friends, and their familiar surroundings, and it was not comfortable. However, there was an enduring hope: God promised that the exile would end.

When you are ready to move on, say, **God promises to be with us even in times of exile, and that our exile will not last forever.**

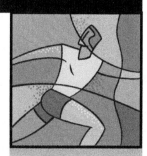

Home Stretch

OPTION 2 (OLDER YOUTH)

Discuss what happens in exile.

Share the following true story by reading it aloud, distributing copies, or projecting it:

Many people think that the Hmong people came to North America to enjoy the economic benefits, but most of them came to escape persecution carried out by the governments of Laos and North Vietnam in retaliation for Hmong support of the United States during the Vietnam War. For many years, the Hmong people fought bravely to slow the advance of the North Vietnamese into Laos and South Vietnam. Thousands of their fighter pilots died on missions that ultimately saved thousands of American lives. Even though the Hmong were allies of the United States, the U. S. pulled out of Vietnam without doing anything to protect them against the terrible revenge that has been directed toward them, including chemical and biological warfare. Many Hmong people ended up in refugee camps in Thailand, where they continued to endure abuse. Some have managed to come to the United States—not to seek a free ride, but to seek life. Hmong refugees in North America struggle with our unusual ways. They are very willing to adapt and learn, but it has been difficult. Many people show real bigotry towards the Hmong people without realizing how they got here.[1]

Ask, **Do you know any people with Hmong heritage?** There are sizable groups of people with Hmong heritage in Wisconsin, Minnesota, California, and other states. Explain the following effects that people experience when they are exiled (write the terms on the board):

- *Loss of possessions*—The Hmongs and other exiles had to leave home quickly, or lose their lives. There was no time to sell the house and no money to pack up the furniture and ship it. Many exiles leave home with just the clothes on their backs, and the possessions they leave behind are taken by others.
- *Loss of connections*—Family members often become separated from one another during exile. Perhaps the younger members of a family move, but the grandparents are too ill and must stay behind. When fleeing for your life, you go wherever you are able, and sometimes that means different places for different relatives.
- *Loss of identity*—People who are exiled in a foreign country often find that their culture and traditions clash with their new society. They are expected to speak a new language and fit in with new social customs. The way of life that identified the exiles before grows weaker over time and eventually disappears.

Emphasize that people in exile are especially glad to hear a message of hope and a future—a message such as the one that Jeremiah preached.

When you are ready to move on, say, **God promises to be with us even in times of exile, and that our exile will not last forever.**

1. Information obtained from http://www.jefflindsay.com/Hmong_tragedy.html on 1-25-2016..

Finish Line

Note:

Don't forget to distribute copies of the Portable Sanctuary to students before they go.

OPTION 1 (LITTLE PREP)

Give thanks for what you have.

Distribute to students copies of "What They Have" (Reproducible 2) or show it as a projection. Review together the information comparing and contrasting the conditions in which the different peoples of the world live. Spend extra time on any statistics that are of particular interest to your students. After you have looked through the entire handout, ask, **How do these facts and figures make you feel?** As residents of North America, we are truly blessed. Even the poorest among us have more than the majority of the world's citizens. The point here is not to make your students feel guilty for what they have but to make them thankful for it, and to make them sensitive to the needs of those around us and around the world. God calls us to be his hands and feet in the meeting of those needs.

Close the session in prayer, giving opportunity for students to express their thanks to God for the many blessings and the hope he has given them.

OPTION 2 (MORE PREP)

Grow where you're planted.

Explain that Jeremiah's encouragement of the people in exile could be termed "Grow where you're planted." This means that God invites us to give our best in—and to make the best of—whatever situation we might currently find ourselves in. This doesn't mean that we shouldn't take a stand against injustice or work to make things better; it does mean that God can use us and bless us wherever we find ourselves now, and that God's promise to give us hope and a future can sustain us during the tough stretches of life's journey.

Bring to class seeds for tomatoes, squash, or other edible plants. Find a place to plant these seeds and invite class members to help you do so. Work together to tend the plants in the coming weeks. When the fruits or vegetables are ready for harvest, take the produce from your plants to a food bank, a homeless shelter, or another organization that ministers to people in exile.

Close the session in prayer, giving opportunity for students to express their thanks to God for the many blessings and the hope he has given them.

> *Note:*
>
> Don't forget to distribute copies of the Portable Sanctuary to students before they go.

Carnac's Clues

Instructions: Cut apart the clues in the right-hand column and seal each one in an individual, numbered envelope. Unless you can memorize the answers in the left-hand column, you will need to have them stashed somewhere, written on your palm, or something similar.

Answer	Question
1. Sis boom bah.	1. Describe the sound made when a sheep explodes.
2. The La Brea Tar Pits.	2. What you have left after eating the La Brea Tar Peaches.
3. U-C-L-A, A-F-L, C-I-O.	3. How do you spell ucaliflicio?
4. Fondue.	4. What do you get on your Fon if you leave it out all night?
5. Spam.	5. Describe the sound of a pig hitting the bottom of an elevator shaft.
6. Blood sugar.	6. What should a vampire cut down on when he's on a diet?
7. Cyclone.	7. What do you call the clone of a guy named "Cy"?

What They Have

How do these facts and figures make you feel?

- At least 80 percent of humanity lives on less than ten dollars a day.[1]

- Nearly a billion people entered this century unable to read a book or sign their names.[2]

- The richest 20 percent of the world's population accounts for three-quarters of world income.[3]

- The vast majority of the world's hungry people live in developing countries, where 13.5 percent of the population is undernourished.[4]

- There are 795 million undernourished people in the world today..[5]

- Poor nutrition causes nearly half (45%) of deaths in children under five—3.1 million children each year.[6]

- Every year, 2.6 million children die as a result of hunger-related causes.[7]

- The number of seniors experiencing hunger increased by 88 percent between 2001 and 2011.[8]

- Sub-Saharan Africa is home to 43 percent of the global poor.[9]

- Almost three-fifths of the world's extreme poor are concentrated in just five countries: Bangladesh, China, the Democratic Republic of Congo, India, and Nigeria.[10]

Sources:
1. http://www.globalissues.org/article/26/poverty-facts-and-stats
2. Ibid.
3. Ibid.
4. http://www.bread.org/who-experiences-hunger
5. http://www.wfp.org/hunger
6. http://www.wfp.org/hunger/stats
7. Ibid.
8. Ibid.
9. http://www.compassion.com/poverty/poverty.htm
10. Ibid.

Portable Sanctuary

Day 1

Tough News

"Which do you want first—the good news or the bad news?" Perhaps you've heard this question asked as part of a joke. But maybe someone has asked you this *seriously*. So, which do you choose? Do you prefer to get the bad news out of the way first, saving the "treat" of the good news for last? Would you rather hear the good news first, so that you'll be "pumped up" before hearing the bad news? We never like to get bad news, but when some good news accompanies it, the bad news can be a little easier to take.

Questions and Suggestions

- Read Luke 2:21–35. How do you think Mary and Joseph felt about this news from Simeon? How would Mary's soul be pierced?
- Whenever you have to bring bad news to someone, how could you also bring some good news?
- Pray.

Day 2

Blessed to Be a Blessing

Most of the differences between animals and humans are obvious. One difference that is often overlooked is in the ways we share. When you're eating dinner and your dog is sitting there begging, you might give the dog a morsel from the table. But give your dog a whole, freshly-cooked hamburger some time. The dog will not eat half and then nudge the other half toward you. The dog will gulp down the whole thing, barely even chewing it. When food is placed in front of a dog, the dog's sole

---

Questions and Suggestions

- Read Acts 7:54–60. Stephen had just given his testimony before an infuriated crowd that was determined to kill him. How did he respond to these angry people? How did he feel about going "home" to be with Jesus?
- What are the comforts and good things of home that you will miss most? What good things would you like to make a part of your own home?
- Pray.

N O T E S

focus is on getting as much as possible, as quickly as possible. As human beings made in the image of God, something inside of us knows that when we are blessed with something, it is good to share that blessing with others—even when we ignore or suppress that feeling.

- Pray.

Questions and Suggestions

- Read Genesis 12:1–3. Why did God bless Abraham? How has the entire world—down to this very day—been blessed through Abraham?
- Are you "territorial"—strictly guarding what is yours, or do you share your blessings with others? What do you think God wants from you in this area?
- Pray.

Day 3
Perspective

A *stereogram* is a computer-generated image that looks like a bunch of random dots at first glance, or maybe like a repeated pattern. But after you stare at the page for a while, a "hidden image" emerges. When we see something in print, our eyes are trained to look at a single plane—the sheet of paper or the computer screen, for example. The hidden image can only be seen when you train your eyes to focus *beyond* the plane surface. Some people can do this pretty easily, while others can never seem to get it. It's all a matter of perspective.

Questions and Suggestions

- Read Luke 2:36–38. Anna had waited perhaps sixty years or more for the One who would redeem the people of God. Do you think she ever got tired of waiting?
- Check out http://www.vision3d.com/sghidden.html for some cool "hidden image" pictures.
- Pray.

Day 4
The 100% Prayer

How many prayers do you think go up to God each day—each second of each day? How many of those prayers are heart-felt and ask for good things? God, please heal my grandfather. God, please help my parents get back together. The reality is, we live in a broken world, where disease hurts and kills. Sometimes God miraculously heals, and sometimes he does not heal physically. We also live with God-given free will that God has chosen not to violate—even if it means that two people choose to divorce. But when we lay down our own wills and our efforts to manipulate and control life and the world around us, God answers by giving us hope and a future with him. That prayer is answered yes—100 percent of the time.

Questions and Suggestions

- Read 2 Corinthians 12:7–10. Paul repeatedly asked God to remove the "thorn" in his flesh. How did God answer? How did Paul respond?
- Have you prayed the "100% prayer" to God? If not, what is stopping you? If so, how has God's grace been working in your life since that time?
- Pray.

Day 5
Coming Home

Someday you will spread your wings and leave the nest of home, flying out into the great unknown. Your faith, your home life, and your schooling all contribute to help you be ready for that day. If your home life has been a happy and supportive one, you will fondly look forward to times when you get the chance to come home. It may be your mom's cooking, your dad's funny stories, or your comfy bed. When you have experienced a good home, there's nothing quite like coming back for a stay.

UNIT THREE

INTRO

Responding in Righteousness

This unit will look at how we can have hope in life no matter what the current circumstances, due to the promise of God's unfailing love. We will also look at our responsibility in our relationship with God—to turn away from things that keep us from growing closer to him and to commit ourselves to living as holy, blameless children of God. You will also explore how God continues to pursue us even when we have turned away; he doesn't want any of us to be separated from him for eternity. The unit will conclude by encouraging your students to be prepared for the return of Jesus Christ.

The presence, the power, and the promises of God in our lives call for a response on our part—a response of righteousness.

Unit 3 Special Prep

SESSION 1—WARM UP, Option 2 (More Prep), calls for copies of a connect-the-dot puzzle. STARTING LINE, Option 1 (Younger Youth), requires rope and a variety of everyday items; you can also use an actual yoke. For Option 2 (Older Youth) you can use the Digital BRIDGES CD, a computer, and a data projector. FINISH LINE, Option 2 (More Prep), calls for old T-shirts and an outdoor area with dirt.

SESSION 2—For WARM UP, Option 1 (Little Prep), you can use candy or another small prize. Option 2 (More Prep) requires small tombstones created with plaster, wood, or paper, and markers. STARTING LINE, Option 1 (Younger Youth), calls for two tin cans and a very long string. THE TURN requires a story of someone who confessed but then fell back into sin. HOME STRETCH, Option 1 (Younger Youth), calls for a glass jar, water, food coloring, and bleach. FINISH LINE, Option 1 (Little Prep), requires envelopes.

SESSION 3—WARM UP, Option 1 (Little Prep), calls for some outrageous stories, made up before class. Option 2 (More Prep) requires the Balderdash board game. For STARTING LINE, Option 1 (Younger Youth), you can use candy or another small prize. FINISH LINE, Option 2 (More Prep), calls for earplugs and loud music.

SESSION 4—For WARM UP, Option 1 (Little Prep), you can use candy or other small prizes. Option 2 (More Prep) requires long lengths of yarn and a small prize. STARTING LINE, Option 1 (Younger Youth), calls for several items that can be tossed or juggled; you can also invite a guest juggler to visit the class. Option 2 (Older Youth) requires phone access, person(s) whom you can call, and person(s) who can call you. FINISH LINE, Option 2 (More Prep), calls for dirty pennies, lemon juice, vinegar, salt, water, a plastic bowl and spoon, and paper towels.

Leading into the Session

Warm Up

Option 1 — LITTLE PREP
Create a chair shortage.

Option 2 — MORE PREP
Connect the dots.
Copies of a connect-the-dots puzzle, pencils

Starting Line

Option 1 — YOUNGER YOUTH
Illustrate being yoked together.
Rope, a variety of everyday items; actual yoke (optional)

Option 2 — OLDER YOUTH
Discuss: What are you yoked to?
Reproducible 1, pens or pencils; Digital BRIDGES CD, computer, and data projector (optional)

Leading through the Session

Straight Away

Explore the Bible passages.
Bibles

The Turn

Look closer at salvation.
Bibles, Reproducible 2, pens or pencils

Leading beyond the Session

Home Stretch

Option 1 — YOUNGER YOUTH
Discuss the blessings of family.

Option 2 — OLDER YOUTH
Wait quietly for the Lord.
Bible

Finish Line

Option 1 — LITTLE PREP
Turn the other cheek.

Option 2 — MORE PREP
Mourn as Jeremiah did.
Bible, old T-shirts, outdoor area with dirt

SESSION 1

GOD IS GOOD

Bible Passages
Lamentations 3:25–33, 55–60

Key Verse
The LORD is good to those whose hope is in him, to the one who seeks him.
—Lamentations 3:25

Main Thought
God gives us hope in life—even during the tough times.

Along with the Song of Songs, Esther, Ruth, and Ecclesiastes, the Hebrew Bible includes the Book of Lamentations in a collection called the "Five Scrolls." Each of these books played a key role in the liturgical life of ancient Judaism. Of the five it is Lamentations that is clearly tied to a specific historical event in the life of Israel: the destruction of Jerusalem and subsequent exile in 587 BC.

No other event burned itself into Israel's memory with the searing depth of the fall of Jerusalem. The power of this memory rested in part on the fact that Jerusalem's fall undermined some elements of Israelite worship. Psalms 46, 48, 76, 84, and 87 illustrate the manner in which the royal theology had shaped aspects of Israel's liturgical life. These "Songs of Zion" focused on the glory of the city and its temple in the belief that they, like the Davidic monarchy, would last forever. Devastation and exile demonstrated such beliefs and the worship they underwrote to be false. Faced with the raw reality of the destruction of their most sacred places, the survivors of this ancient holocaust were faced with a choice. On one hand they could question all the old promises of God. Was Israel indeed God's chosen people? Did Jerusalem have any real status? Was the Lord indeed God? On the other hand the survivors could find a way to express their deep grief over unimaginable loss—but do so in the determined hope that God was not finished with them and that restoration was still possible and would eventually come. Lamentations was the articulation of this second alternative.

The Book of Lamentations is a series of five poems, four of them acrostics, lamenting the collapse of Jerusalem in the language of worship. It is important to understand that these poems were for the *public* expression of Israel's grief. They were songs for the corporate worship life of those who had to go on even in the face of crushing defeat and loss. Acrostic is a literary device where each stanza or line of the poem begins with a successive letter of the alphabet. It was employed particularly with songs of lament as a structural way of saying that the singers' grief was complete, not unlike the sense of the English language idiom, "from A to Z." Lamentations 1, 2, and 4 each have twenty-two verses, one for each letter of the Hebrew alphabet. The third poem, or chapter 3, contains sixty-six verses. Here each letter of the alphabet introduces three lines of poetry. As it would be nearly impossible for an English translation to follow this pattern without contrived artificiality, it has rarely been attempted.

Walter Brueggemann explores the work of Old Testament scholar Kathleen O'Connor and finds there a description of Lamentations as encouraging or expressing five acts: an act of grieving "truthfulness" to the situation and to God, "an act of impassioned hope" in the face of the near complete absence of God, "a wish for justice" that pleas the wrong that has been done to the community, an act that gives moral shape to that community, and an act that promotes human agency and thus the acceptance of responsibility for our situation and our future."[1] Concludes Brueggemann, "The Book of Lamentations knows, from the ground up (and down), that history does not happen so easily as hegemony [those in power] might imagine. History happens, rather, in the midst of silence that is at the edge of absence. It happens first of all in tears that are long and salty, that yield only late, very late, to hope."[2]

1. O'Connor's work is quoted at length in Brueggemann, *An Introduction to the Old Testament: Canon and Christian Imagination* (Louisville: Westminster John Knox Press, 2003), 337–339.
2. Ibid., 343.

OPTION 1 (LITTLE PREP)

Create a chair shortage.

Before class remove most of the chairs from your meeting room so that there will not be enough for all students. Stash the extra chairs out of sight. If any arriving students ask about the shortage of chairs, explain that they were needed for another purpose. Encourage students without chairs to sit on the floor, the table, or wherever they can. Once you are ready to begin, ask, **What are some of the basic things you expect when you come to this group?** People usually expect that your group will begin and end at certain times and that you will study the Bible. Mention any other "regular elements" to your group (singing, prayer, goodies, and so forth). If your group has some sort of covenant agreement, this would be a good time to explain it. If you frequently use off-the-wall ideas with your group, your students may not ever know what to expect! Point out that students also expect to have a place to sit when they come. Bring out the extra chairs so that everyone has a place to sit.

Say, **When things are not as you expect, it can really disrupt your day—or your life!**

Warm Up

> *Note:*
> If you sent the Portable Sanctuary home with students last week, take some time at the beginning of this session to review and discuss their experience.

. . . .

OPTION 2 (MORE PREP)

Connect the dots.

Bring to class copies of a connect-the-dot puzzle. These can be easily found in children's activity books or even on the Web at places such as www.activitypad. com/dot-to-dot.html. Distribute a copy to each student to complete; if you wish, you can have a contest to see who finishes first.

Point out that life can be sort of like a dot-to-dot puzzle—a really complicated one! As we move from point to point, we're looking for a clearer picture to emerge. Sometimes it takes a while for things to come together. And sometimes things don't come together in the way we expected.

Say, **When things do not turn out as you planned, it can really disrupt your day—or your life!**

Starting Line

OPTION 1 (YOUNGER YOUTH)

Illustrate being yoked together.

Bring to class a long rope and a variety of representations of everyday things or people that students might be "yoked" (committed) to. Some suggestions are as follows:

- Part of a computer (representing the Internet)
- A cell phone (representing friends and music)
- A valentine or a wrapped gift (representing a boyfriend or girlfriend)
- A hymnal (representing church)
- A framed family photo (representing family)
- A Bible (representing God)
- A dustpan and a broom (representing a job)
- Several bricks (representing anything else that students might be yoked to)

Ask for a volunteer to come forward. Explain that in life we are all "yoked" to certain things—that is, we have an obligation or commitment to them. Tie the rope around your volunteer's waist and tie the objects to him or her one at a time, explaining what they represent. As you or your students think of some other examples, tie on some bricks for good measure. Help your students to understand that some things might occupy our time or cost us money but we are not yoked to them. For example, I am not obligated to attend a movie or watch television. However, if I have purchased a cell phone, then it cost me money—money that is wasted if I do not use it; and if I have a job, I am expected to show up for work. Ask your volunteer to walk around after he or she is "yoked" to all of these things. Point out that the more things we are yoked to, the more difficult it is to get around. If possible, bring an actual yoke for students to see; explain that this is an "attachment point" for an ox or other animal that is pulling a load.

Say, **Let's see what God thinks about the things we are yoked to.**

OPTION 2 (OLDER YOUTH)

Discuss: What are you yoked to?

Distribute copies of "What Are You Yoked To?" (Reproducible 1) or show it as a projection. If you have access to a computer and data projector during class time, you can let students try the "Balancing Act" game on the Digital BRIDGES CD.

After giving students some time to think, discuss together the different things that we are yoked to in life. Some suggestions might include the Internet, a cell phone, a boyfriend or girlfriend, music, friends, church, family, God, and a job. Help your students to understand that some things might occupy our time or cost us money but we are not yoked to them. For example, I am not obligated to attend a movie or watch television. However, if I have purchased a cell phone, then it cost me money—money that is wasted if I do not use it; and if I have a job, I am expected to show up for work. Point out that the more things we are yoked to, the more difficult it is to get around.

Say, **Let's see what God thinks about the things we are yoked to.**

Explore the Bible passages.

Read together Lamentations 3:25–33 and 55–60. Explain that the authorship of Lamentations has traditionally been credited to the prophet Jeremiah (who wrote the book right before this). Jeremiah lived in a tough time. The capital city, Jerusalem, had been destroyed by the Babylonians and the people had been killed, tortured, or taken captive. There was a strong mood of defeat and despair. Jeremiah was honest about the fact that disobeying God invites disaster, but he also knew that God suffers when his people suffer and that all hope was not lost.

Discuss the following questions:

Straight Away

- **What is a "lamentation," or what does it mean to "lament" something?** To lament means to express sorrow, mourning, or regret for something, often aloud or in a demonstrative fashion. Ask students what kinds of things we might lament today. We can lament the death of a loved one, the loss of a relationship, the pain of someone's hurtful words, the consequences of our poor choices, and so forth.
- **This chapter is an acrostic poem; the stanzas begin with successive letters of the Hebrew alphabet. Why would anyone write a chapter in this way?** Students may feel that this was a technique to help memorize or remember the chapter. A more likely explanation is that this was a structural way of saying that the composer's (or reader's) grief was complete, sort of like our idiom "from A to Z."
- **What do you think it means to "wait quietly for the salvation of the LORD"? Does this mean no talking in church, or something else?** Point out that to a people in captivity who had seen their city destroyed and their family members and friends tortured and killed, there would have been a strong urge to take revenge or to fight their way to freedom. Jeremiah advised the people to wait patiently for God instead of taking things into their own hands.
- **Why is it better to "bear the yoke" (burden) while we are young?** As we age we tend to lose our strength; we are better able to handle strenuous tasks while we are young. These verses also indicate that there was a lesson for these people to learn through their suffering; it was better for them to learn it now than to wait. When we are young we are more open to instruction and not so "set in our ways."
- **In the middle of this terrible situation, where did Jeremiah find hope?** God does not reject us forever; even though he may bring us grief at first, his love and compassion will prevail. In fact, God does not want to see us suffer. When we hurt, God hurts.
- **What does it mean to be "in a pit" in life?** A pit is a low place, a trap, a situation that you can't change no matter how hard you try. Discuss with your students times when they have felt absolutely stuck, with no hope. How long did they have to wait? How did things finally get better?
- **Jeremiah wrote about "their vengeance" and "their plots." Whom was he talking about?** This would have referred to the Babylonians; however, it could apply to any person or situation that is making us miserable. Jeremiah saw any insult to the people of God as an insult to God himself. Point out

that there is a difference between suffering insult from others because we are Christians and suffering the consequences of poor choices or wrong actions.

- **What are some of the things you think God wanted these people—and wants us—to learn?** Invite students to respond. We have already seen that the people were pretty weak on justice and righteousness, so now they had time to think about those things. This would also have been a good time for the people to learn patience as they were in a "pit"—someplace where they couldn't change things no matter how they tried.

Say, **Even though the people had turned away from God, they held onto the promise of God's love and compassion.**

The Turn

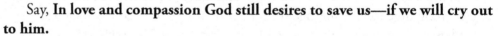

Look closer at salvation.

Distribute copies of "Salvation Word Study" (Reproducible 2) and give students time to complete the handout, or show it as a projection and work on it all together. Ask for those who are willing to share their thoughts with the rest of the class.

Point out that the concept of salvation has grown and developed somewhat over time. In Genesis 32, Jacob asked God to save him from the wrath of his brother, Esau. In Exodus 14, the Lord saved the entire Israelite nation from the Egyptians. In Lamentations, Jeremiah held out hope that God would save the people from their suffering in captivity. When we study the New Testament, we see that salvation was thought of in more of a spiritual sense. Jesus taught that we should seek salvation for our souls, and Paul developed this idea further. Encourage your students to pursue the spiritual salvation that Jesus offers—but not to rule out the other ways that God can (and does) save.

Say, **In love and compassion God still desires to save us—if we will cry out to him.**

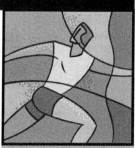

OPTION 1 (YOUNGER YOUTH)

Discuss the blessings of family.

Say, **When we are going through tough times as Jeremiah and his people were, the care of our families or special friends can make all the difference in the world.** Divide the class into groups of three or four and ask the members of each group to share with one another about persons in their families that they are thankful for and why. Who is always willing to listen? Who is always there for them when they are down? Who challenges them to give their best? Who loves them unconditionally as Christ loves us? Encourage students to think outside the limits of their biological families. Perhaps they have guardians, special friends, or members of the church who are a special blessing to them.

Share with the whole class about someone in your life who is special to you and why. Explain that Jeremiah didn't have to go through his struggles alone; other people were there to share the burden—and the hope that God would help them.

When you are ready to move on, say, **In the name of God, this group is here to celebrate the good times with you—and to walk with you through the tough times.**

Home Stretch

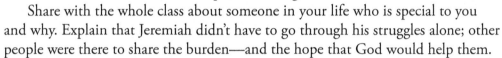

OPTION 2 (OLDER YOUTH)

Wait quietly for the Lord.

Don't say anything for a minute—just look at your students. Break the silence by pointing out how uncomfortable we are with silence. It would be difficult to find a time or place in our day for silence even if we wanted to, but we are accustomed to surrounding ourselves with noise—music, television, cell phones, pagers, even the "written noise" of e-mail and instant messenger. Read aloud 1 Kings 19:11–18. Say, **God often speaks in a whisper or in the quiet times. If we're never still, how will we hear him?** Challenge your students to spend a few moments in silence, waiting quietly for the Lord and seeking to sense his presence and his voice. Encourage class members to incorporate silence and waiting into their regular times of prayer.

When you are ready to move on, say, **When we wait quietly for God, we can be ready to hear what God has to say.**

131

Finish Line

OPTION 1 (LITTLE PREP)

Turn the other cheek.

Ask, **Does anyone know what the phrase "turn the other cheek" means?** This is a reference to the teaching of Jesus in Matthew 5:38–42. Explain that this lesson may be one of the most difficult for us to follow. After all, if someone strikes us, isn't it our right to strike back? At some points Jesus seemed to relax the Law in order to come closer to its intent, but in this case he actually strengthened the Law.

Ask your students to think of the people in their lives with whom they have the greatest conflict. Perhaps this would include a bully at school, a sibling at home, a parent, a teacher, or a supervisor at work. Now challenge class members to commit to "turn the other cheek" to these people during the coming week. Emphasize that this does not mean setting yourselves up for abuse; it *does* mean that you will respond to these people calmly and in love, giving what they ask and even more. Ask, **Why would God have us put up with something we don't deserve?** Sometimes we suffer because of our own bad choices; but when we suffer voluntarily, God can increase our faith and teach us new things—and God can work through our suffering to help others.

Close the session in prayer, thanking God for the hope he brings—even during the tough times.

Note:

Don't forget to distribute copies of the Portable Sanctuary to students before they go.

OPTION 2 (MORE PREP)

Mourn as Jeremiah did.

Refer again to Lamentations 3:29, where Jeremiah exhorted the people to bury their faces in the dust. Ask, **Was Jeremiah advising us to be more like ostriches?** Explain that Jeremiah was referring to the mourning process that was common at the time. This included putting dust on one's head or throwing dust in the air, shaving one's head, tearing one's clothes, and sitting in sackcloth and ashes. (See Job 1:20; Job 2:12; and Luke 10:13 for examples of these rituals.) There was also a strong element of repentance to this ritual, of seeking God's mercy not only for one's suffering but also for the forgiveness of one's sins. Ask, **What rituals do we observe today when we are in mourning?** It is still common in North America to wear black, to fly flags at half-mast, and to stay in seclusion, limiting contact or socialization with others.

Distribute old T-shirts to students to put on over their regular clothes. Take the group outdoors to a field or other location with plenty of dirt. Give students the opportunity to tear their T-shirts and to throw dirt in the air. Even if this seems strange to them, explain that in Jeremiah's time it was a clear way to show that you were very sad, that you were very sorry for what you had done, and/or you were passionately calling out to God for help. Encourage any students who are going through a time of grief or guilt to use this opportunity to cry out in their hearts for God's help.

Close the session in prayer, thanking God for hearing your cries and for the hope he brings—even during the tough times.

What Are You Yoked To?

If you are yoked to something, then you have an obligation or commitment to it. What are some of the people or things you are yoked to in your life?

Salvation Word Study

When you hear or see the word *salvation,* what comes to your mind?

_____

_____

What things have you been saved from in your life?

_____

_____

How have you been an agent of salvation in the life of someone or something else?

_____

_____

Salvation means deliverance from danger or difficulty; when used in a spiritual sense, *salvation* means deliverance from the power or the penalty of sin. In its original Koine Greek language, the New Testament word for *salvation* is *soteria* or *soterion.* It can also mean *Savior*—the one who brings salvation.

Look up the following references to *salvation* to see how the concept has grown and developed over time:

• Genesis 32:9–12 _____

• Exodus 14:29–31 _____

• Lamentations 3:25–27 _____

• Matthew 10:28 _____

• Romans 1:16 _____

Portable Sanctuary

Day 1

Yoked Together in Love

Have you ever listened to the vows during a wedding? The bride and groom often promise to be committed to one another "for better or for worse, for richer or for poorer, in sickness or in health, 'till death do us part." What the couple is really saying (even if they don't stay true to it) is that they will love one another regardless of what comes along in life. In other words, they are "yoked together in love." We can't keep this kind of commitment in our own strength—but in God's love, it can be done.

Questions and Suggestions

• Read 1 John 4:10–12. When has someone in your life shown you abundant, undeserved love? How did you respond? How have you seen God in the love of others?

• Examine your life. Who is showing the love of God to you? Whom can you show the love of God *to?* Pray about it.

Day 2

True Joy

Relationships often break up because the two partners become frustrated with one another. It starts gradually at first, but then communication breaks down—and when it does happen, the words are filled with anger and frustration. Jesus came to communicate fully to us the Father's love and the Father's will. The more we understand this, the more complete our joy in the Lord will be. God does not leave us guessing. He shows us how to truly love—and makes it possible for us to do so.

Questions and Suggestions

- Read John 15:9–17. When have you walked out of a great relationship and been sorry later? How committed are you to remaining in the love of Christ?
- Ask God to maintain your joy even when things aren't going as you might like.

Day 3
God's Peace

The human mind is amazing. People have discovered or invented things such as penicillin to treat infections and the Internet to provide communication. Knowledge is increasing at an exponential rate. And yet, human beings cannot find true peace without God. People try to do it with possessions, food, sex, drugs, and other things. But real peace can come only from God. Those who have found this peace know that it is better than anything else they could ever have in life.

Questions and Suggestions

- Read Philippians 4:4–7. Why would Paul repeat his command to rejoice? What does God's nearness have to do with rejoicing?
- God wants to give you his peace. Where are you struggling with peace in your life? Ask God to give you his peace and he will.

Day 4
Got Patience?

When you know what's going on, it's easy to have patience. Do you remember going on a trip when you were little? Maybe you were going on vacation or to someplace special. You were dying the whole way in the car, wanting to know when you would be there—but your parents just kept on driving. They knew how long it would take, and that you still had a way to go. When you know the way, it's easy to have patience. But even when we don't know all the details of our journey, we can still have patience—if we can trust the One who is driving.

Questions and Suggestions

- Read Proverbs 14:29. When have you showed patience and it really helped you out? When have you showed a lack of patience and it really hurt things?
- What are some areas where you need to have more patience? Ask God to help you grow in these areas.

Day 5
Got Self-Control?

It is a sign of wisdom—and maturity—to be able to say "no" to some things. Your parents probably taught you early on not to get in cars with strangers. They knew that children can be bribed easily with candy. If you put out too much food every day for some dogs, they will eat and eat until they get so overweight that they die. One of the blessings of walking with God is that God teaches us—and helps us—to say "no" to things that are harmful to us and to others.

Questions and Suggestions

- Read Titus 2:11–14. What are some specific examples of "ungodliness and worldly passions" that you can think of?
- Think about areas where you lack self-control. Turn those over to God and ask for God to help you with them. God will!

Leading into the Session

Warm Up

Option 1 Unscramble the acrostic.
LITTLE PREP *Reproducible 1, pens or pencils; candy or another small prize (optional)*

Option 2 Create your own tombstone.
MORE PREP *Small tombstones created with plaster, wood, or paper; markers*

Starting Line

Option 1 Make a telephone.
YOUNGER YOUTH *Two tin cans, very long string*

Option 2 Discuss jumping off a cliff.
OLDER YOUTH

Leading through the Session

Straight Away

Explore the Bible passages.
Bibles

The Turn

Discuss repenting and turning away.
Story of someone who confessed but then fell back into sin

Leading beyond the Session

Home Stretch

Option 1 See how repentance is cleansing.
YOUNGER YOUTH *Glass jar, water, food coloring, bleach*

Option 2 Discuss personal responsibility.
OLDER YOUTH

Finish Line

Option 1 Write a letter to yourself.
LITTLE PREP *Reproducible 2, pens or pencils, envelopes*

Option 2 Incorporate your students into the church body.
MORE PREP *Chalkboard or dry erase board, paper, pens or pencils*

SESSION 2

REPENT AND LIVE!

Bible Passages
Ezekiel 18:4, 20–23, 30–32

Key Verse
I will judge you, each one according to his [or her] ways, declares the Sovereign LORD. Repent!
—Ezekiel 18:30

Main Thought
Each of us is responsible for his or her own actions.

The prophet Ezekiel was a contemporary of Jeremiah. Ezekiel also focused his attention on the Babylonian crisis that played out in Jerusalem shortly before and after the city's destruction. Isaiah, Jeremiah, and Ezekiel all focused on Jerusalem's destruction, interpreting it in the light of God's presence in Israel's life and thus understanding these events as moments of divinely authorized judgment and, beyond punishment, hope for the future.

Unlike Isaiah and Jeremiah, Ezekiel was among those transported to Babylon, where he delivered his message to the exiles and shared their situation. His prophetic call occurred in "the fifth year of the exile of King Jehoiachin" (1:2) "in the land of the Chaldeans [Babylonians] by the River Chebar" (1:3, NRSV). From these references scholars conclude that Ezekiel was among the residents of Jerusalem marched into exile in the first deportation of 598 BC. From 2 Kings 24:10–17 we learn that Nebuchadnezzar laid siege to Jerusalem and deported segments of the population including King Jehoiachin and most of the political and religious leadership. This was the first deportation. Eleven years later, after Zedekiah attempted to throw off the Babylonian yoke, Nebuchadnezzar's army returned, this time to destroy the city and deport an additional segment of the population. If we situate Ezekiel's ministry within this chronology, we will see that he began preaching to exiles before their hope of return was crushed by the news of Jerusalem's fall. Chapters 1—24 of the Book of Ezekiel are concerned with the final judgment about to fall on the city; chapters 25—48 focus on its hope for restoration.

Ezekiel seems to have been influenced more profoundly by the priestly tradition of which he was a member. Jeremiah also was a priest and likely Isaiah as well, but within the Book of Ezekiel there burns an unusually strong awareness of the holiness of God. For Ezekiel, judgment signaled by the Babylonian crisis meant that the holy Lord God of Israel could no longer live in the midst of a people so profaned and corrupted by sin as the citizens of Jerusalem. Thus the theme of God's holiness and the requirement that Israel live in a corresponding holiness are profoundly carried out in the Book of Ezekiel.

Texts such as chapter 18 readily explain why Ezekiel has often been described as the "prophet of individual responsibility." But to think of the message of Ezekiel in such universal human terms runs the risk of neglecting the immediate context of that message. It is important to understand Ezekiel as a priest with a pastor's heart. He preached a message that offered counsel, comfort, and hope to a dejected people. "Ezekiel 18 is a summons to failed Israel to repent and return to Torah obedience."[1] As such, this chapter is not an appeal to a moral individualism where each person is accountable for himself or herself. Rather, "when taken locally and pastorally … the body of the text is organized into three generations: the first generation of a righteous man (vv 5–9) [that of the good king Josiah], the second generation of a wicked man (vv 10–13), [the bad king Jehoiakim], [and] the third generation of a righteous man (vv 14–18) [the generation of King Jehoiachin of which Ezekiel and the exiles were part]."[2] Through historical events verdicts of acquittal and conviction had already been announced for the first two generations, but the jury was still out for the exiles. Would they use the bitter experience of exile as a time of cleansing, repentance, and renewal—or would they waste the opportunity by thinking of themselves as chained to the sins of the previous generations?

1. Walter Brueggemann, *An Introduction to the Old Testament: Canon and Christian Imagination* (Louisville: Westminster John Knox Press, 2003), 206.
2. Ibid.

OPTION 1 (LITTLE PREP)

Unscramble the acrostic.

Distribute copies of "Acrostic Scramble" (Reproducible 1) and give students time to complete the handout. If you wish, you can award candy or another small prize to the person who finishes first. Correct answers are as follows:

Warm Up

P The Macy's Day <u>Parade</u> is held each Thanksgiving in New York.

E I like bacon and <u>eggs</u> for breakfast.

E Did you vote in the last <u>election</u>?

T <u>Turkey</u> is often eaten on Thanksgiving Day in the U.S.

N That's my <u>name</u>—don't wear it out!

R Roses are <u>red</u>, violets are blue.

A

N

D

V <u>Valentine's</u> Day is February 14.

I Eskimos live in <u>igloos</u>.

E <u>Electricity</u> can be very shocking!

L Four <u>laps</u> around the track makes one mile.

<u>R E P E N T</u> and <u>L I V E</u>

Say, **Today we will talk about what it means to repent and live.**

• •

OPTION 2 (MORE PREP)

Create your own tombstones.

Bring to class enough small, blank tombstones for each student to have one. These could be the plaster type purchased from a novelty store, or something made out of wood or even paper.

Distribute the tombstones and markers and ask, **When you die, what do you want your tombstone to say about you?** Invite students to write their own epitaphs. What do they want to be remembered for when their lives are over? This is a great opportunity to discuss the fact that we will each face death someday; we should be ready for that time, and we should also have the right priorities during our time on this earth. Ask students who are willing to share what they wrote. Point out that the messages on people's tombstones talk about who they were and what they did—not about the personalities or accomplishments of others.

Say, **Today we will talk about the responsibilities that each of us carries in life.**

> *Note:*
>
> If you sent the Portable Sanctuary home with students last week, take some time at the beginning of this session to review and discuss their experience.

139

Starting Line

OPTION 1 (YOUNGER YOUTH)

Make a telephone.

Bring to class two empty tin cans and a very long piece of thick string, yarn, or twine. Poke a hole in the end of each can, thread one end of the string through, and knot it so that it doesn't slip out. Invite two volunteers to separate the cans so that the string is taut. If you can do this so that one person is outside or in another room, it will add to the effect of this activity.

Ask a student to speak into one of the cans, as the person on the other end of the string listens to his or her can. Now, shout to the person on the other end, **Did you hear the message?** There is some transmission of sound through this sort of "telephone" but it is obviously not as effective as the real thing. You can invite different volunteers to try this experiment. Point out that sometimes we get the wrong message in life. Sometimes the other person is not communicating clearly, or we're not doing a good job of listening. Sometimes we make wrong assumptions, and someone needs to clear things up for us.

When you are ready to move on, say, **Let's look at a time when God cleared up a misunderstanding his people had.**

· ·

OPTION 2 (OLDER YOUTH)

Discuss jumping off a cliff.

Ask, **Have your parents ever been displeased with the influence that one of your friends was having on you and said, "Well, if Jimmy or Susie jumped off a cliff would you do it too?"** Explain that this is a rhetorical question; the obvious and implied answer is *no*. Ask, **What are your parents really trying to tell you when they ask this annoying question?** They are saying to take responsibility for yourself; don't just mindlessly follow what other people say or do. Discuss with your students the attempts that many people make to ditch responsibility for their own actions. Sometimes people say in kidding, "The devil made me do it," but people really do blame lots of things for their actions: the way they were raised, heredity, the media, even the lyrics of songs! Other people and things do influence our thoughts and behavior, but there has to be a point where we take responsibility for our own actions.

When you are ready to move on, say, **Let's see what the prophet Ezekiel had to say about personal responsibility.**

Explore the Bible passages.

Read together Ezekiel 18:4, 20–23, and 30–32. Discuss the following questions:

Straight Away

- **Fathers and sons belong to God—but what about mothers and daughters?** They are included too. The point here is that the totality of the human race—*every* member—belongs to God.
- **What is "fatalism"?** Fatalism is the belief that something is bound to happen no matter what you do, sort of like being cursed. Explain that Ezekiel's people were suffering from a sort of fatalism; they believed that they were being punished by God because of what previous generations had done. This can lead to a sense of irresponsibility; if you think you're cursed anyway, why even try?
- **Could this work in the opposite (good) way?** Yes; people could also assume that just because their parents were blessed by God, they will also be blessed no matter what they do. We see this in people who grow up and rarely worship God or even think of God, yet they feel spiritually safe because their parents went to church and served God.
- **What was Ezekiel saying about responsibility here?** You are responsible for your own actions—including your own sin. Even wicked people, if they turn from their sin and do right, will live; God will not hold their past sins against them. Point out that we do feel the effects—good or bad—of the lives of our parents and ancestors, but God does not hold us responsible for what our parents do or do not do. Each of us is responsible to God for his or her own life.
- **What did Ezekiel mean about the person who sins dying? Don't we *all* die?** Each of us will die a physical death someday. Ezekiel was referring to spiritual death—eternal separation from God.
- **What does God think about our past sins when we turn from them? What should we think about them?** See verse 22. God forgets about our past sins when we repent (turn away) from them. (See also Psalm 103:11–12 and Jeremiah 31:34.) If God does not hold these against us, then we shouldn't, either. Encourage your students to learn from the past but to rest in God's forgiveness—not continuing to beat themselves up by saying, "I did this" or "I did that."
- **How does God feel about the punishment or death we receive because of our sin?** Remind your students that we were all created by God—whether we acknowledge God or not—and we all belong to God. God takes no pleasure in seeing anyone die—even a wicked person! Instead, God is pleased when we wake up, stop living for ourselves, and choose life.
- **God urges his people not to die. Why would anyone willingly choose death?** God has created in each of us the basic instinct of survival. When our lives are threatened, we seem to find superhuman strength; we do what it takes to survive. Some people choose physical death due to depression or an altered mental state. Some choose death for a greater cause, such as defending a nation or saving loved ones. Others choose death almost passively, as the result of self-gratifying behaviors or addictions such as smoking, drinking, or overeating.

Say, **In the Spirit of God, Ezekiel urged the people to repent and live.**

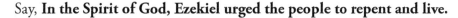

141

The Turn

Discuss repenting and turning away.

Without using names, share about someone you know who publicly confessed sin but then was caught doing the same thing again. (For example, a young teenage girl ended up pregnant. She gave her heart to Christ and started coming to youth group. The teens and others in the church loved her and supported her and her new baby. About a year later, she was pregnant again—and this time one of the guys in the youth group was the father.) Ask your students to share (again, without using names) their own stories of people going back to something they had turned away from. Ask, **If you say you're sorry but then go back to doing what you said you were sorry for, have you really repented? Didn't Jesus say we should forgive someone "seventy-seven times" (Matthew 18:21–22)?** Allow your students to honestly wrestle with the tension among the concepts of forgiveness, accountability, repentance, and responsibility.

Say, **Repentance is about more than just saying you're sorry. It's about a change of heart—and a change of ways.**

Home Stretch

OPTION 1 (YOUNGER YOUTH)

See how repentance is cleansing.

Bring to class a large glass jar, food coloring, and bleach. Fill the jar about ¾ of the way with water. Say, **Call out to me some different sins that many teenagers struggle with.** As students make suggestions, put a drop of food coloring in the water for each one. If you use various colors of food coloring, the water will begin to turn black. Now say, **When you repent of your sin and turn to Christ, he is faithful to cleanse you from that sin.** As you say this, begin to pour bleach into the water until the water is clear again. Say, **The more completely we are filled with Christ, the better defense we have against sin in the future.** As you say this, add some more drops of food coloring to the water; because of the presence of the bleach, the color will continue to disappear.

When you are ready to move on, say, **Jesus wants to do the same cleansing in your life—if you'll let him.**

Note:

You may want to practice this experiment beforehand in order to perfect your technique.

OPTION 2 (OLDER YOUTH)

Discuss personal responsibility.

Ask, **Is personal responsibility a good thing or a bad thing?** Invite students to respond. If I am responsible only for myself and my own decisions, it can bring great freedom and simplicity to my life. However, taking this philosophy too far can make us selfish—we live only to serve ourselves and don't care how it affects others. This is the polar opposite of God's intent for the body of Christ, the church—we are to serve others first.

Present the following "spiritual responsibility removers" to your students and discuss each:

- The government tells me when, where, and how I can (or can't) pray, read the Bible, or worship.
- My parents' faith is all that matters. If they are in good with God, then so am I.
- My thoughts and actions make no difference to God; he loves me, and I'll go to heaven no matter what I do (or don't do).

Allow your students to honestly wrestle with the tension among the concepts of personal responsibility, selfishness, community, and eternal security.

When you are ready to move on, say, **God has given each of us personal responsibility—and we can be supported in that responsibility through others in the church.**

Finish Line

OPTION 1 (LITTLE PREP)

Write a letter to yourself.

Distribute to the class copies of "Where Will I Be?" (Reproducible 2) and envelopes. Invite students to write letters to themselves expressing what they want their walks with God to be like in a year. Say, **We've talked a lot today about our accountability to God. What is God saying to you? What things in your life need to change so that you can experience more fully the life God has for you? Is there anything you need to repent and turn away from?** If you have some in your class who haven't yet made that decision to follow Christ, challenge them to think about it and to imagine what things could be like in a year if they made the decision. (See "Leading a Teenager to Christ" in the back of this book.) After students have had time to finish their letters, ask them to put the letters in their envelopes, to seal them, and to write their names and the date a year from now on the envelopes. Students should put these somewhere safe where they will not lose them but can open them up in a year and see what God is doing in their lives.

Close the session in prayer, asking God to give you the full life that comes when we repent and turn to him.

OPTION 2 (MORE PREP)

Incorporate your students into the church body.

Say, **Ezekiel didn't give any "minimum age" for our responsibility to God. You are all old enough to carry that responsibility.** Brainstorm together with your students about ways they can take responsibility in your congregation. Are there service opportunities that are unfilled? Are there needs for new ministries that could be started by your group? Find out the minimum age requirement for participating in the business meetings of your church and encourage your eligible students to do so. Encourage your students with 1 Timothy 4:12: "Don't let anyone look down on you because you are young, but set an example for the believers in speech, in life, in love, in faith and in purity." Write suggestions on the board as they are made, and ask a student to summarize these on paper.

Close the session in prayer, thanking God for the responsibility and growth you see in your students.

Note:

Don't forget to distribute copies of the Portable Sanctuary to students before they go.

Acrostic Scramble

Fill in the blanks below with the correct answers. The first letters of the answers will form a scrambled acrostic. Unscramble the acrostic to discover the theme for today's session.

____ The Macy's Day _____ is held each Thanksgiving in New York.

____ I like bacon and _____ for breakfast.

____ Did you vote in the last _____ ?

____ _____ is often eating on Thanksgiving Day in the U.S.

____ That's my _____—don't wear it out!

____ Roses are _____ , violets are blue.

A

N

D

____ _____ Day is February 14.

____ Eskimos live in _____ .

____ _____ can be very shocking!

____ Four _____ around the track makes one mile.

____ ____ ____ ____ ____ ____ and ____ ____ ____ ____

Where Will I Be?

We've talked a lot today about our accountability to God. What is God saying to you? What things in your life need to change so that you can experience more fully the life God has for you? Is there anything you need to repent and turn away from?

When you are finished writing your letter, put it in an envelope, seal it, and write your name and the date a year from now on the envelope. Put the envelope somewhere safe where you will not lose it but can open it up in a year and see what God is doing in your life.

Dear _____,
        (your name)

_____

_____

_____

_____

_____

_____

_____

_____

_____

_____

_____

Portable Sanctuary

NOTES

Day 1

Taming the Tongue

We sometimes fail to understand how powerful our words are. A cruel insult can hurt just as much as a punch in the gut—even more! And a compliment or word of praise from someone else can set us to floating on cloud nine. When a stream of gossip pours from our mouths, reputations can be destroyed. But when praise and intercession flows from our lips, the joy of the Lord abounds and lives are changed. We are responsible for taming our tongues—and this responsibility is a very important one!

Questions and Suggestions

- Read James 3:3–12. When have someone's words been a blessing to you? When have they cut like a knife?
- How is your "tongue control"? Do you have a problem with gossiping, lying, telling dirty jokes, or laughing at someone else's expense? Pray that God will give you a consistent—and tame—tongue.

Day 2

Conformed or Transformed?

Conforming is a forced action. If we lock someone up in prison, he has to function within his captivity and do what the guards say. Most of the time we conform to something because we have to. But transformation is a different thing altogether; it means a change on the inside. A student can conform to the requirements of a class just to get through it, not learning much of anything. But a student who is transformed by a love for the subject being studied will be changed forever.

Questions and Suggestions

- Read Romans 12:1–2. How does this passage expand our usual idea of worship? It would be nice to know God's will—how can we do that?
- Do people see a difference (transformation) in you, or are you like everyone else around you (conformed)? Examine your heart and ask God to begin a transformation in you.

Day 3
The Summary of Love

Have you ever heard of *CliffsNotes*? They were booklets that summarized the content of major novels. In the days prior to the Internet, some students tried to avoid reading whole books by using just the *CliffsNotes* to write their book reports. (They usually received an *F* when they did this.) *CliffsNotes* books were not there to help people get around knowing the books; they were designed as a *summary* of what had been read. Love is sort of like the summary of God's law: if you will just love your neighbor as yourself, the rest will come back to you.

Questions and Suggestions

- Read Romans 13:9–10. How do the commandments listed all flow from "Love your neighbor as yourself"? Who is your neighbor?
- Thank God for his deep and eternal love for you. And remember, we have to give in order to receive.

Day 4
A Pleasing Faith

You can have faith in lots of things—faith in the sun to rise tomorrow, faith in your mom to have dinner waiting when you get home, faith that the chair you're sitting in will not collapse. But there is a kind of faith that is special—a faith that is pleasing to God. This is not some "dream faith" that is impossible to attain or that only Bible heroes had. This faith is currently possessed by people all over the world and even in your own church. Do you know it when you see it?

Questions and Suggestions

- Read Hebrews 11:5–6. What kind of reward is this talking about?
- By definition, faith is not always easy—after all, it means believing in something you can't necessarily see! Ask God to give you a faith that is pleasing to him.

Day 5
Purity Begets Purity

Do you know anyone who has it good and things just seem to be getting better, a person who succeeds at every task, who just can't seem to do wrong? This same sort of thing can happen in our walk with God. When we live lives of purity, then more purity grows in us, and it surrounds us. When we are growing in purity, we show that we know God. If we are growing in corruption—impaired integrity or lack of right living—then it is clear that we don't know God.

Questions and Suggestions

- Read Titus 1:15–16. When have you seen purity in your life blossom into more purity? When have you seen corruption develop into more corruption?
- God calls us to live pure lives—physically, mentally, and spiritually. Ask God to root out any sources of corruption in your life.

Leading into the Session

Warm Up

Option 1
LITTLE PREP
Tell some whoppers.
Some outrageous stories, made up before class

Option 2
MORE PREP
Play a game of Balderdash.
Balderdash board game

Starting Line

Option 1
YOUNGER YOUTH
Discuss learning your lesson.
Reproducible 1, pens or pencils; candy or another small prize (optional)

Option 2
OLDER YOUTH
Discuss "shades of truth."

Leading through the Session

Straight Away

Explore the Bible passages.
Bibles

The Turn

Discuss God's eternal Word.

Leading beyond the Session

Home Stretch

Option 1
YOUNGER YOUTH
Think about helping the lost.
Chalkboard or dry erase board

Option 2
OLDER YOUTH
Commit to speaking the truth.

Finish Line

Option 1
LITTLE PREP
Pray for desolate lands.
Reproducible 2, pens or pencils

Option 2
MORE PREP
Unstop your ears!
Earplugs, loud music

SESSION 3

RETURN TO GOD

Bible Passages
Zechariah 1:1–6; 7:8–14

Key Verse
"Return to me," declares the LORD Almighty, "and I will return to you," says the LORD Almighty.
—Zechariah 1:3

Main Thought
Even when we have turned away from God, God pursues us and invites us to return.

Bible Background

In the year 539 BC Israel's long, dreary years of exile came to an end. Her Babylonian masters were themselves overthrown by a new power in the region, the empire of the Medes and Persians. Established and led to power by Cyrus, the Persian Empire treated its subject peoples with a much gentler hand than the Babylonians. There was no question who was in charge, but within the framework of Persian power small people groups such as the Jewish exiles enjoyed more freedom than had previously been the case. After conquering Babylon it was Cyrus who decreed that the exiles could return to Jerusalem and Judah, which became a political unit within the empire. This was the "Persian period" of Israel's history, the era of Nehemiah, governor of Judah, and Ezra, the great interpreter of Torah. It was also the period of the three post-exilic prophets—Haggai, Zechariah, and Malachi. During this period the theme of prophecy in Israel changed from judgment to restoration, and Zechariah's writings are a fine example of that shift.

The Book of Zechariah opens with verses that locate the prophet's call early in the reign of the Persian emperor Darius, roughly 520–516 BC. In other words, this prophet began preaching soon after the exiles began returning home. Upon their arrival they found Jerusalem in ruins, the once great temple a heap of rubble and the once protective walls mere piles of stones. If the city of David was to enjoy a safe and coherent life again it would have to be reconstructed from the ground up. The same could be said for Jerusalem's religious life. Different voices argued for different agendas to guide the nation's spiritual renewal. Some assumed that return from exile meant a return to things as they had been before Jerusalem's fall, with a king who was both a religious as well as political figure. Others thought that the Babylonian crisis was God's judgment on the institution of monarchy and that new leadership was needed. These voices advocated the priestly class as the source of leadership for a new community founded on a more explicitly religious footing. Still others, and here we find the towering figure of Ezra, located Judaism's health in obedience to Torah. This great emphasis on Torah as Israel's foundation led to the rise of a new class of religious leader, the scribe or "teacher of the Law." Ezra was a priest for sure, but he did not function in Jerusalem as a performer of sacrifices or worship leader. Rather, he was the one who brought with him from Persia the scrolls of Torah and who was the key figure in their public reading and interpretation. By this process Torah and its interpretation became the new basis for life in post-exilic Judaism.

The prophecy of Zechariah carries several of these themes. It expresses a concern for priestly leadership, but also stands in the tradition of insisting on Torah obedience. In this latter emphasis Zechariah anticipated the work of Ezra, who arrived in Jerusalem after the years of Zechariah's preaching. So we need to understand Zechariah's work as a determined effort to shape the life of post-exilic Jerusalem according to the teaching of Torah. For Zechariah the direction of that life was an open question as the exiles struggled to rebuild their lives and community. He delivered a series of prophetic sermons that reminded the exiles of the previous generation's shortcomings so they could be avoided. Zechariah declared that the key to Jerusalem's future blessing and a peaceful life with God lay in the rejection of the wicked ways of the past.

OPTION 1 (LITTLE PREP)

Tell some whoppers.

Before class, make up some outrageous stories about things that happened to you or that you participated in. Make the stories so incredible that they will be suspect from the start. The exact details are not important. You may wish to begin by saying, **You'll never believe what happened to me this weekend!** Tell the stories with dramatic flair and without using notes. After students have laughed at you and rejected your fanciful tales, ask, **What are the craziest things you've ever been through—things so amazing or so terrible that you'll never forget them?** Invite students to respond.

After everyone has had a chance to share, say, **Times of great joy or great tragedy can change the course of our lives.**

Warm Up

• •

OPTION 2 (MORE PREP)

Play a game of Balderdash.

Bring to class the Balderdash board game. In this game, players try to make up authentic-sounding definitions for obscure words. Instead of keeping score, allow students to use the cards to make up definitions for several different words. After a few minutes, ask, **Does anyone know what the word *exile* means?** To be in exile means to be forced or kicked out of your own home or country. Explain that the people of ancient Judah were exiled for many years—taken captive and separated from their homes and their families, many of them feeling as if God had deserted them.

Say, **The exile was a tragic event—it changed the lives of the people of Judah forever.**

Note:

If you sent the Portable Sanctuary home with students last week, take some time at the beginning of this session to review and discuss their experience.

OPTION 1 (YOUNGER YOUTH)

Discuss learning your lesson.

Distribute to students copies of "Lesson Learned" (Reproducible 1) or show it as a projection, and allow students time to complete the assignment. After time has elapsed, review the correct answers together:

Starting Line

1.—d. To have an obligation or commitment to that person or thing.
2.—c. Jeremiah.
3.—a. A poem where the stanzas begin with successive letters of the alphabet.
4.—c. In the fact that God does not reject us forever; his love and compassion will prevail.
5.—b. Ezekiel.
6.—b. The belief that something is bound to happen no matter what you do.
7.—d. We are each responsible for our own actions—including our own sins.
8.—c. Both of the above.

If you wish, you can award candy or another small prize to the student who gets the most correct answers.

Ask, **What does it prove if you got all the questions right on this little quiz?** It shows that you've been in class the past two weeks and paid attention to what was being discussed—that you've "learned your lesson." Point out that life is full of tests—times where we can see whether or not we have learned anything from our past experiences.

When you are ready to move on, say, **Let's see what Zechariah had to say about the people learning their lesson.**

· ·

OPTION 2 (OLDER YOUTH)
Discuss "shades of truth."
Ask, **What does the phrase "shades of truth" mean?** This describes a belief that one can partially, or almost, tell the truth. Invite students to give examples of "shades of truth." Some possible answers are as follows:

- You've finished your math homework but not your history homework. When your mom asks if your homework is done, you say yes, knowing that you're referring only to your math while your mom thinks you mean the whole thing.
- You want to go on a date with someone but your parents forbid it. You tell them you're going to spend the night at a friend's house, and you do stay at your friend's—after going out on the date.
- Fudging a little on my time card or cheating on a test is not nearly as bad as stealing merchandise from the company or vandalizing the school.

Point out that if we are not truthful at all times, then others will not know when they can trust us. It is also important for us to *receive* the truth. An alcoholic who will not accept others telling him he has a problem will drink himself to death. The truth is sometimes difficult for us to hear or to choose—but it can make a huge difference in our lives.

Say, **Let's see how Zechariah proclaimed the truth to his people.**

Straight Away

Leading through the Session

Explore the Bible passages.
Read together Zechariah 1:1–6 and 7:8–14. Discuss the following questions:

- **How would you summarize Zechariah's words in chapter 1?** Zechariah was saying, "Your parents and grandparents blew it! God kept telling them through the prophets to straighten up. But they wouldn't listen. Your ancestors are all dead now and so are the prophets—but God's words are still true! Learn the lesson and return to me—don't make the same mistake your parents did!"
- **When have your parents made decisions that negatively impacted you?** Invite students to respond. Examples might include the decision

152

of a mother to have an affair, the decision of a father to quit a job, or the decision of parents to rack up credit card debt that is now overwhelming the family. The point here is not to decide whether the decisions were right or wrong but to talk about how those decisions affected your students. Discuss honestly the fact that some decisions seem to have *no* good alternatives.

- **According to Zechariah, how did the people finally respond to God's warnings and the tragedy that came?** They repented, realizing that they got exactly what they deserved. Remind your students that repentance means a change of heart and a change of lifestyle. The people stopped trying to defend their choices or come up with excuses, and admitted, "We were wrong."

- **In chapter 7, what were God's specific instructions to the people?** To be people of justice and mercy, looking out for widows, orphans, aliens, and the poor. Emphasize that this theme—taking care of the powerless, of those who cannot care for themselves—runs throughout the Old Testament prophets (many of whom you have been studying over the past weeks). This is not some private, personal, "warm-feeling-inside" religion—it's taking action to care for others on God's behalf.

- **How was it that the people did not "hear" God's instructions?** The text says that they refused to pay attention or listen and had "stopped up their ears" and made their hearts hard (7:11–12). Help your students to understand that the people weren't deaf; this indicates that they *chose* not to listen. God was not taking issue here with people who had never heard him or heard *of* him; he was calling to account people who both heard him and knew him—and should have known better.

- **What did God mean when he said that he "scattered" the people?** This is a reference to the Exile—foreigners coming into Judah, destroying the towns, and hauling the people off as slaves. Through the prophets, God had been trying for years to get the people's attention. Through invading armies, God finally got their attention.

- **When have you been a part of a group that was tragically "scattered"?** Invite students to respond. Perhaps someone has been a part of a group of friends that was very close, but the others moved away or there was a falling out. Perhaps your congregation has been through a "split," where a large group of people left to start their own congregation or to attend another church. Discuss honestly the pain of being scattered or exiled, whether it comes from avoidable causes or could not be helped.

- **These are some pretty negative passages! Where was the hope in all this?** In 1:3, God promised to return to the people if they would return to him. God made it clear that the people were the ones who walked away from the relationship and that he was inviting them back—but they would have to take action.

Say, **Even though the people had turned away from God, God pursued them and invited them to return.**

The Turn

Discuss God's eternal Word.

Say, **Some of you have English lectures that seem eternal. You've all been on trips that seemed eternal. How is God's Word—his words and decrees—eternal?** Invite students to respond. Emphasize that there is a lot to "unpack" from this one tiny statement! If God is eternal and all-powerful, then his words are also eternal. We know that Jesus is God's Word and that he has been with God from the beginning (John 1:1–2). People come and go, but God—and God's Word—outlasts them all.

Ask, **How *could* we respond to an eternal word—and what would the results of our response be?** Some people dismiss God's Word as untrue—but it always proves to be right on. Others feel that God's Word is irrelevant—but the Bible is by far the most popular book of all time. Some people defy God's Word, only to have to face the reality of that Word sooner or later. If God's Word is eternal and not going to change, then we are better off to accept it and deal with it.

Now ask, **Can you think of anything else that is really eternal?** Invite students to respond. Our souls might go on eternally, but they haven't been around since the beginning of time. God created the universe, and we know that it will come to an end someday. There are some pretty long-term things around—but nothing that has always been and always will be—as God is.

Say, **If you want to live forever, placing your faith in God's eternal Word is the wise choice.**

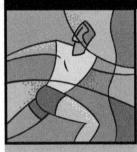

Home Stretch

OPTION 1 (YOUNGER YOUTH)

Think about helping the lost.

Invite students to share about times when they have been lost. How did they feel when they realized that they were lost? How did it feel to be found again? Ask, **Is it possible to be around people—even people you know—and still be lost?** It is possible to be lost in a crowd or in a crowded place, and it is possible to be around people you know and still feel very alone. Write on the board the different scenarios that are suggested. Ask any students who are relatively new to your group to share about their first experiences as a part of your group. Did they feel "lost" at first? Was it easy or difficult to be accepted or assimilated into your group? Say, **Just as the people of Judah felt lost and alone in a foreign land, there are people all around us today who feel lost and alone.** Ask students to suggest ways that they can help the "lost" around them, as you write their suggestions on the board.

When you are ready to move on, say, **God calls to the lost and seeks the lost—and he works through you and me to help the lost.**

OPTION 2 (OLDER YOUTH)

Commit to speaking the truth.

Say, **Zechariah took a risk when he boldly spoke God's truth. How do people sometimes respond when we speak the truth?** The truth does not always bring about positive reactions. People are not happy when it upsets their way of life or when it exposes their lies. Ask, **Why might the truth not be easy to *give*?** Invite students to respond. If the truth is going to hurt someone or cause a confrontation, we might hesitate to speak it. Ask class members to share some good principles that you, as individuals and as a group, can commit yourselves to when speaking the truth. Some possible answers are as follows:

- Speak the truth *in love*. Make sure you are motivated out of genuine concern and not looking for revenge.
- Make sure you have your facts straight, so that the truth you share is actually the truth.
- Speak the truth privately. People do not usually appreciate being "called out" in front of others.
- Be positive in your presentation. Find some compliments to share along with your truth, instead of launching into a list of "what's wrong."
- Before you even speak, ask yourself, "Is what I am about to say true? Is it positive? And is it necessary?" If you can answer yes to all three questions, then you will probably stay away from gossip.

When you are ready to move on, say, **Speaking the truth, in love, can bring healing and wholeness into the lives of others.**

OPTION 1 (LITTLE PREP)

Pray for desolate lands.

Distribute to students copies of "Desolate Lands" (Reproducible 2) or show it as a projection and allow a few minutes to complete the assignment. Ask, **Where in our town or area are there "desolate lands"—places that are run-down, where spirits are low, or where all hope seems to be lost?** Perhaps there are neighborhoods that have been abandoned by churches or businesses or where there is a desperate need for the love of God; maybe your students know of some families that could really use God's peace; or maybe some of your students themselves feel "desolate" right now as they struggle with important relationships or heavy issues. Identify together some local "desolate lands" and spend some time praying for these places, asking God to make you and your students heralds of his truth and of his call for all to come to him.

Close the session by praying for any special needs your students may have.

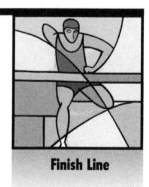

Finish Line

Note:

Don't forget to distribute copies of the Portable Sanctuary to students before they go.

155

OPTION 2 (MORE PREP)

Unstop your ears!

Note:

Don't forget to distribute copies of the Portable Sanctuary to students before they go.

Distribute earplugs to your students (the roll-up foam-type will work best) and ask them to insert the earplugs into their ears. After everyone's ears are "stopped up," play some music, very softly at first. Increase the volume slowly until a student can tell what song is playing. Continue to increase the volume until *all* students can hear the song well. Now ask everyone to remove their earplugs; the music will be deafening! Turn the volume down to an acceptable level and ask class members to notice the details in the music they couldn't hear with the earplugs in. Point out that we can still hear with our ears stopped up—but not very well! When we unstop our ears, we can hear details that we totally missed before. Say, **God is speaking truth into each of your lives. If you can't hear it, you need to check to see what is blocking the sound.**

Close the session by praying for your students to hear clearly the voice of God in their lives, and by praying for any special needs that may be represented.

Lesson Learned

Instructions: Choose the best answer for each question below in the time allotted.

1. What does it mean to be "yoked" to someone or something?
   (a) To share bacon and eggs together.
   (b) To think that someone or something is funny.
   (c) To have affection for that person or thing.
   (d) To have an obligation or commitment to that person or thing.

2. Who probably wrote the Book of Lamentations?
   (a) Joshua
   (b) Jesus
   (c) Jeremiah
   (d) Lamentiah

3. What is an acrostic poem?
   (a) A poem where the stanzas begin with successive letters of the alphabet.
   (b) A poem that is constructed like a crossword puzzle.
   (c) A poem that expresses anger.
   (d) A poem that expresses joy.

4. In the middle of tragedy, where did Jeremiah find hope?
   (a) In his bank account.
   (b) In cookie dough ice cream and old Chicago records.
   (c) In the fact that God does not reject us forever; his love and compassion will prevail.
   (d) Jeremiah didn't find any hope in the middle of tragedy.

5. Who wrote the Book of Ezekiel?
   (a) Moses
   (b) Ezekiel
   (c) Jeremiah
   (d) None of the above.

6. What is "fatalism"?
   (a) Devotion to an apparition of Mary that occurred at Fatima, Portugal.
   (b) The belief that something is bound to happen no matter what you do.
   (c) An obsession with time.
   (d) The belief that you are likely to become overweight.

7. What is the main theme of Ezekiel 18:4, 20–23, and 30–32?
   (a) Children are punished for the sins of their parents.
   (b) The Messiah would soon come into the world.
   (c) The Exile was about to be over.
   (d) We are each responsible for our own actions—including our own sins.

8. What does it mean to repent?
   (a) To have a change of heart.
   (b) To change your ways.
   (c) Both of the above.
   (d) None of the above.

Desolate Lands

Where in your town or area are there "desolate lands"—places that are run-down, where spirits are low, or where all hope seems to be lost? Maybe you know of a neighborhood that has been abandoned by churches or businesses or where there is a desperate need for the love of God; maybe you know of a family that could really use God's peace; or maybe your own life feels "desolate" right now as you struggle with important relationships or heavy issues. Identify some local "desolate lands," write them below, and spend some time praying for these places, asking God to make you a herald of his truth and of his call for all to come to him.

Portable Sanctuary

Day 1

Spiritual "To Do" List

Years ago, Tim McGraw released a song called "Live like You Were Dying." It talks about a man who finds out that he has cancer. Faced with his own death, the man begins to figure out what's really important in his life. He reads the Bible. He spends more time with his family. He takes time to enjoy God's creation by going skydiving and mountain climbing. When we understand how short our lives on this earth are, we will also take a good look at our priorities.

Questions and Suggestions

• Read 1 Peter 4:7–11. How would you summarize this spiritual "to do" list in your own words?

• Ask God to help you set the right priorities in your life.

Day 2

Judge Not

Have you ever been to a court proceeding, or seen one on television? The standard by which the case is decided is the law. It's the judge's job to know the law—to know what it says, what it means, and how to apply it. As the Creator of the universe, God knows the laws of the universe. He even knows the human heart, better than we know ourselves. We can leave it up to the eternal Judge to decide where each of us stands. And each of us will someday have to give account before that Judge.

Questions and Suggestions

- Read Romans 14:10–13. Is it better to bow to God and confess to him now, or later? Why?
- Is there someone you have judged lately? Ask God to forgive you, to change your attitude about this person, and to give you more compassion for him or her.

Day 3
Justice for All

Sometimes the world just doesn't seem fair. In North America, things are pretty good. Even the poorest among us are better off than much of the rest of the world. We can worship as we please and express our opinions as we please. In some countries there's not enough food to go around, and you can be arrested just for worshiping God or for speaking out against the government. Different countries have different standards—but in God's eyes all people everywhere can know God's justice.

Questions and Suggestions

- Read Isaiah 42:1–4. How can Jesus be gentle and still bring justice? What kind of justice is this talking about?
- Pray that God will use you as an agent of God's justice on this earth—right where you live.

Day 4
Truth, Spoken and Heard

God calls us not only to be willing to speak the truth, but to also hear the truth. When we are dealing in truth and only truth, we don't have to wonder, "What is that person's motivation? What will that person think of me?" We know what that person thinks because he or she has said it plainly. And we don't have to "beat around the bush"—we can talk about the real issues and get to the real solutions. The key in all this truth speaking (and hearing) is *love*.

Questions and Suggestions

- Read Ephesians 4:11–16. Do you feel comfortable speaking the truth to the people you know—even when it might hurt?
- When we see a friend stumbling, it is our responsibility to speak truth to that person. Ask God to give you courage when you are faced with this type of situation.

Day 5
Growing Up

Before Jesus was crucified, he was put on trial before Pilate, the Roman governor. Pilate saw the truth—Jesus was not guilty of any crime. But instead of making a stand for the truth, Pilate allowed the pressure of the crowd to overcome him, and he had Jesus crucified. Pilate may have symbolically washed his hands of the situation, but the guilt was still there. You will probably never face a decision like Pilate's—but each of us faces decisions that have significant consequences to them.

Questions and Suggestions

- Read Matthew 27:11–26. Pilate was appointed to his position by the Roman government, not by the Jewish citizens. Why do you think he gave in to the crowd?
- Have you ever been faced with a difficult situation and weren't sure what to do? Ask God to give you wisdom and strength in these times. This is part of growing in Christ and taking on the responsibility of truth.

Warm Up

Option 1
LITTLE PREP
Solve a word scramble.
Reproducible 1, pens or pencils; candy or other small prizes (optional)

Option 2
MORE PREP
Play Follow the Yarn.
Long lengths of yarn, small prize

Starting Line

Option 1
YOUNGER YOUTH
Juggle your priorities.
Several items that can be tossed or juggled; guest juggler (optional)

Option 2
OLDER YOUTH
Give and receive messages.
Phone access, person(s) whom you can call, person(s) who can call you

Leading through the Session

Straight Away

Explore the Bible passages.
Bibles

The Turn

Discuss looking for Christ.

Leading beyond the Session

Home Stretch

Option 1
YOUNGER YOUTH
Think about a "weary Lord."
Bible, chalkboard or dry erase board

Option 2
OLDER YOUTH
Discuss the world's need for healing.
Chalkboard or dry erase board

Finish Line

Option 1
LITTLE PREP
Pray for God's refining fire.

Option 2
MORE PREP
Practice refining.
Dirty pennies, lemon juice, vinegar, salt, water, plastic bowl and spoon, paper towels

SESSION 4

HERE COMES THE SON

Bible Passages
Malachi 2:17 — 3:5; 4:1–3

Key Verse
"See, I will send my messenger, who will prepare the way before me. Then suddenly the Lord you are seeking will come to his temple; the messenger of the covenant, whom you desire, will come," says the LORD Almighty.
—Malachi 3:1

Main Thought
Christ came to bring people to God — and will come again.

Bible Background

Running through the prophetic books of the Old Testament is the theme of "the day." Typically this is the "day of the Lord," *yom Yahweh* in Hebrew. Before the destruction of the northern kingdom and later the fall of Jerusalem, the popular understanding was that the day of the Lord would be one of blessing. It would usher in the realization of God's direct rule on earth and thus, Israelites assumed, the time when they would live comfortably and take their ease. It would also be a time when their enemies ceased to threaten them. Beginning with Amos, however, many of the prophets turned the tables on this line of thought. They declared that the day of the Lord would be one of darkness and not light. "It will be," said Amos, "as though a man fled from a lion only to meet a bear" (5:19). The post-exilic prophet Malachi continued to use the idea of "the day" in a series of messages that bring the Christian Old Testament to a close.

As with most of the prophets who make up the "Book of the Twelve," little or nothing is known of Malachi, whose name means "my messenger." He was active in Jerusalem during the Persian period after the exiles' return but before the arrival of Ezra. The initial euphoria of homecoming had evaporated in the harsh reality of the multiple tasks confronting the exiles. The city and temple lay in ruins. Houses that had escaped destruction during the invasion deteriorated while thy sat vacant or became the habitat of wild animals. Fields and vineyards were reclaimed by the desert. The exiles faced the enormous challenge of rebuilding their lives from the ground up and, perhaps inevitably, in such a difficult situation the faith of some began to fail. Faced with decisions between rebuilding shelters for themselves or the house of the Lord the exiles chose the former. Malachi was preceded by the prophet Haggai, who had preached strong sermons against those who made this choice; the temple had to be the first priority of a rebuilt Jerusalem. Malachi's sermons or oracles also took the stance of calling the city to religious and ethical duty as the first responsibility of its settlers.

The Book of Malachi is structured by a series of messages that take the form of disputes between the prophet and residents of Jerusalem who failed to understand what it was to be the people of God. The point-counterpoint of 2:17 illustrates the dialogue that runs through the book: the prophet says, "You have wearied the LORD with your words," and the people ask, "How have we wearied him?" While the focus of these different disputes varies a bit, they mostly deal with "inattentiveness to cultic [worship] requirements, an inattentiveness that profanes, pollutes, and defiles, making Jerusalem inhospitable to Yahweh."[1] As with nearly all of the prophets, even Malachi's harsh words of criticism were balanced by a hope-filled vision that the situation would be resolved. He wrote of "that day" when the Lord would have a righteous people.

The Hebrew Bible does not conclude with Malachi but with Chronicles, which ends with Cyrus' decree that the exiles may return to their homes. By concluding with the Book of Malachi the Christian Old Testament broadens the vision of a hopeful future considerably, looking to "the day" of a righteous people of God and setting the stage for the Messiah who would bring such a reality.

1. Walter Brueggemann, *An Introduction to the Old Testament: Canon and Christian Imagination* (Louisville: Westminster John Knox Press, 2003), 258.

OPTION 1 (LITTLE PREP)
Solve a word scramble.

Distribute to students copies of "Word Scramble" (Reproducible 1), go over the instructions, and allow time for students to complete the assignment. Students can work alone, in pairs, or in small groups. Correct answers are as follows:

Warm Up

semgreens = messenger
reaprep = prepare
rldo = Lord
gekesni = seeking
oemc = come
plemet = temple
vanencot = covenant
ridsee = desire
milgathy = almighty

If you wish, you can award candy or another small prize to the person or team who finishes first or who comes up with the most creative "fill-in" between the words.

Say, **Today you will receive a message—one that has to do with the Lord and his coming.**

Note:
If you sent the Portable Sanctuary home with students last week, take some time at the beginning of this session to review and discuss their experience.

• •

OPTION 2 (MORE PREP)
Play Follow the Yarn.

Bring to class some long lengths of identically-colored yarn. Tie off the pieces close to one another for the starting point; then, merge the strands and run them together over, under, and through different things in the room. Near the end of the strands, separate them and terminate one of the strands at a small prize. See the schematic below:

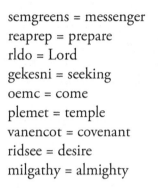

PRIZE

START

Invite a student to pick the strand of yarn that he or she thinks will lead to the prize. The student should then carefully follow that strand to its end. If this strand does not lead to the prize, invite another student to pick a strand and give it a try. (You can do this a third time if necessary.) Point out that many paths in life seem to be leading to the same place—but in the end, all will see clearly what their future will be.

Say, **Sometimes the path of our lives gets confusing—but God is there to help.**

Starting Line

OPTION 1 (YOUNGER YOUTH)

Juggle your priorities.

Bring to class several items that can be juggled or tossed around the room—things such as a ball, a shoe, a stuffed animal, a small pillow, and so forth. Ask for a few volunteers to sit in a circle. Explain to your students that the older they get, the more demands they will have on their time. Suggest something such as a job as you toss one item into the circle and the volunteers toss it around to one another. Suggest additional responsibilities such as college, kids, a house payment, and so forth, tossing in another item for each. Students should attempt to keep all the items moving. If you wish, you can invite someone who juggles to visit the class and to juggle these things as you throw them to him or her one at a time. Even a juggler will eventually be overwhelmed by the sheer number of things to deal with—and so can we, if we're not careful.

When you are ready to move on, say, **Let's see what God has to say about setting our priorities.**

. . . .

OPTION 2 (OLDER YOUTH)

Give and receive messages.

Make arrangements with a person or persons whom you can call during the session and who can call you during the session. Without explanation, make a call, asking the person you speak with to leave a certain message for someone. This person should then call you back and ask to speak with one of your students, asking that student to give a message to another student in your class to call someone. The idea is to get the students giving and receiving messages. Explain to your students that the older they get, the more "messages" they will be asked to listen to in life. Jobs, college, kids, house payments, and other things will all demand their time and attention. It can be difficult to hear clearly the messages that really matter.

When you are ready to move on, say, **Let's see what God did to make his message clear.**

Leading through the Session

Straight Away

Explore the Bible passages.

Read together Malachi 2:17—3:5 and 4:1–2. Discuss the following questions:

- **What things "wearied" the Lord? What was the issue with these things?** The people had lost their sense of right and wrong, seeing no difference between evil people and good people. They also thought that this was "slipping under God's radar"—that God didn't care about it and was not doing anything about it.
- **What do you think 3:1 means? Who was, or is, this messenger?** Invite students to respond. The crucial "coming" of the Lord was the advent of Christ, which was announced by the messenger John the Baptist. (This is

the sense in which the Gospels treat this passage.) Christ has also promised that he will unexpectedly come again. Malachi himself was a messenger of God, letting the people know what God was about to do. As the people of God, we are *all* messengers, spreading the word of God's love.

- **What kind of picture is painted here of the Lord's coming?** Verse 2 rhetorically implies that it would be a difficult day, that the Lord would be like a refiner's fire or a launderer's soap. Help your students to understand the implications of these descriptions. To refine gold or another precious metal is to melt it, allow the impurities to rise to the top, and scrape them away. Gold doesn't even melt until almost 2,000° F! Refining is a hot process, but it purifies, and it is done only to precious or valuable things. Ask your students why they don't bathe with laundry soap; it's because this soap is much more powerful than bath soap and would irritate and damage your skin. The implication is that the Lord's coming would pack a mean punch.

- **Why would anyone *desire* the coming of a day of judgment?** The people expected the "day of the Lord" to bring peace and prosperity back into their lives; they were not expecting to be subjected to judgment. They wanted a pat on the back, but that's not what God had in mind.

- **How are we like metal in need of refining or clothes in need of washing?** Invite students to respond. The metal has value to the refiner and clothes have value—but both are in need of "cleaning up." Point out that we can be just as stubborn as metal when it comes to bending or making changes in our lives, and the sin that we cling so tightly to can be difficult to wash from our lives.

- **According to 3:5, what will be the purpose of the Lord's coming?** It will be for judgment; sorcerers, adulterers, perjurers, cheaters, and oppressors are specifically mentioned. Take time to unpack each of these terms with your students. This is not intended to be an exhaustive list; it indicates that *any* actions contrary to God's standard are subject to God's judgment. In our emphasis on the love and grace of God, we can tend to shy away from the fact that God is the judge of all.

- **Refining is good for gold, and washing is good for clothes—but what will happen to arrogant evildoers in the day of the Lord?** The description is one of total destruction; not a trace will be left of them. Emphasize the use of *arrogant* here; it is the people who think they can defy God and get away with it who will be unpleasantly surprised.

- **Does this description sound like what happened when Christ lived on this earth? How about when he comes again?** Invite students to respond. The image of fire and a furnace sound like common concepts of punishment in hell. The coming of Christ did radically alter the course of this world—although not in the "fiery" ways many were expecting. Point out that when people experienced the healing and the forgiveness of Jesus, they did leap for joy (see Acts 3:1–10). When anyone is confronted with the truth of Christ, he or she makes a choice—a choice to be destined to destruction as the stubble in a field or to experience the healing of the sun of God's righteousness.

Say, **God promised the people that a tough time was coming—but that there would be hope in that day.**

The Turn

Discuss looking for Christ.

Distribute to students copies of "Looking for Christ" (Reproducible 2), or show it as a projection. Allow time for students to work alone, in pairs, or in small groups to complete the assignment. Some possible answers are as follows:

- Everyone in the world does seek peace and satisfaction in life—but not everyone looks for Christ. In fact, many people do not even know that Christ exists. Others know *of* Christ but do not know who he really is or what he offers, so they don't seek him.
- People who decide they want to find Christ look for him through prayer, worship, church services, talking to a pastor or someone whom they consider "spiritual," in nature, by trying to do good deeds and be worthy to meet Christ, by looking for proof that he is real, and even by sending money to television preachers or organizations that promise them that they will receive a miracle from Jesus in that way.
- Students may differ on the best way to find Christ; invite them to share openly. God does promise that we will find him when we sincerely seek him (Jeremiah 29:13).
- Someone who knew exactly when Christ would return could be sure to be ready for that event and to let others know about it. However, such a person could also ignore God until the last minute and then "make the switch." We should live *each* day of our lives as if Christ might return on that day.
- The details of the events that will happen at Christ's return have been the subject of speculation for almost two thousand years. The important thing is for us to know the basics: Christ will return, it will happen unexpectedly, and he will take those who have placed their faith in him to be with him forever.

Explain that we don't need to wait for Christ's kingdom to come because it's already here (Matthew 3:2; 4:17; 10:7; Luke 17:20–21), working in and among us. Instead, we work and pray for the return of Christ (Revelation 22:20). God calls us to be involved in God's redemptive plan—sharing the gospel rather than speculating about the nature and timing of the return of Christ.

Say, **Christ came to bring us to God—and he will come again.**

Leading beyond the Session

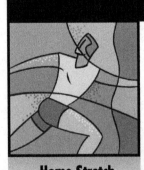

Home Stretch

OPTION 1 (YOUNGER YOUTH)

Think about a "weary Lord."

Read again Malachi 2:17. Ask, **What does a "weary Lord" look like? Does he need to take a break in the middle of his workday? Does he get a headache from answering all those prayers? Or is it something else?** Explain that the sense of weary here is that God's patience is exhausted, that the situation is getting old. Invite students to suggest some other things that might make God "weary" in this way, and to describe some other ways that God might feel when he is "weary" of something. Write students' suggestions on the board. Some possible answers are as follows:

Things that make God "weary"
    People who oppress widows, orphans, and aliens
    War
    Starving children whom no one helps
    Hatred
    Words of praise without accompanying actions

How God feels when he is "weary"
    Sad
    Angry
    Upset
    Disappointed
    Let down

When you are ready to move on, say, **Thinking about the God we love becoming weary shouldn't make us scared—it should break our hearts.**

. . . .

OPTION 2 (OLDER YOUTH)

Discuss the world's need for healing.

Say, **Malachi describes the day of the Lord as coming "with healing in its wings." In what different ways is our world in need of healing?** Write students' responses on the board, pushing class members to go beyond just the healing of physical illnesses. There are relationships in families, between friends, and between nations that need healing; there are attitudes of revenge and hatred that need healing; there are starving children who need healing; there are people addicted to alcohol, drugs, and pornography who need healing. Explain that as bearers of the kingdom of God and the message of God, we can be the ones to carry God's healing to the world—one life and one situation at a time. Point out that the people of Judah suffered in captivity for fifty years, and there are families, towns, and nations in our world that have been in spiritual captivity for at least that long.

When you are ready to move on, say, **The day of the Lord has come and it will come—and it's here right now, with healing for all who will accept it.**

OPTION 1 (LITTLE PREP)

Pray for God's refining fire.

Summarize the session by explaining that the refining fire of God's judgment is hot—but God refines us because he loves us and wants to see the sin purged from our lives. Ask students to consider silently the following questions:

Finish Line

- **Are there things in your life—habits, attitudes, or relationships—that are holding you back from growing closer to God? If so, what are they?**
- **Are you tired of enduring the pain, heartache, and frustration that these things are causing you?**
- **Are you willing to let God refine you, making your life pure and acceptable in his sight?** Remind students that the refining process is not easy—but the end result is well worth it.

Note:

Don't forget to distribute copies of the Portable Sanctuary to students before they go.

Ask students to pair up and to spend some time sharing with one another about the questions you have asked and to pray for one another. Challenge them to check up on one another during the coming week.

. . . .

OPTION 2 (MORE PREP)
Practice refining.

Bring to class ten dirty pennies, lemon juice, vinegar, salt, a small plastic bowl, and a plastic spoon. Mix four tablespoons of lemon juice, eight tablespoons of vinegar, and one teaspoon of salt in the bowl until the salt dissolves. Take a single penny and dip it halfway into the mixture for twenty seconds. When you take it out, students should notice some cleaning effect of the lemon juice/vinegar/salt mixture on the penny. Drop the other nine pennies into the mixture and leave them there for five minutes. Take four of them out and lay them on a paper towel to dry. Take the remaining five pennies out and hold them under running water until they are thoroughly rinsed, laying them out to dry on another paper towel. (*Note:* You may want to practice this experiment beforehand to perfect your technique.)

Point out the differences among the first penny that was just dipped, the four pennies that were laid out to dry, and the other pennies that were rinsed and then laid out to dry. Explain that we all come to God with dirt in our lives. When we seek God's cleansing, we sometimes start the process but then bail out quickly, like the penny that just took a little dip. Sometimes we're like the four pennies that were just laid out to dry—we don't complete the process. But God wants us to go the whole way, giving him every part of ourselves. Remind students that God's cleansing is not easy for us—but the end result is well worth it.

Ask students to pair up and to spend some time sharing with one another about the questions you have asked and to pray for one another. Challenge them to check up on one another during the coming week.

Word Scramble

Instructions: Unscramble the words below, and fill in the gaps between them to see if you can create a message that makes sense.

_____ [**semgreens**] , _____

[**reaprep**] _____ . _____

_____ [**rldo**] _____ [**gekesni**]

_____ [**oemc**] _____ [**plemet**] , _____

_____ [**vanencot**] , _____ [**ridsee**] ,

_____ [**milgathy.**]

Looking for Christ

Does *everyone* in this world look for Christ? Explain. _____
_____
_____

Where and how do people look for Christ? _____
_____
_____

What is the best way to find Christ? _____
_____
_____

Does it matter if we know exactly when Christ will return? Explain. _____
_____
_____

Does it matter if we know exactly what will take place when Christ returns? Explain. _____
_____
_____

Portable Sanctuary

Day 1

Refiner's Fire

After gold and silver are mined from the ground, they are *refined*—they are put into an extremely hot flame until they melt. This causes the impurities in them to separate and float to the top, where they can be removed. We hope we will never experience being physically burned with fire. Sometimes the trials and temptations we go through are very painful too. But the Refiner never lets go, and he never lets us out of his sight. He wants to bring us through the flames as new, pure creations.

Questions and Suggestions

• Read Zechariah 13:7–9. Why would the sheep scatter if the shepherd was hurt? How many "sheep" survived the wrath of God here?

• Pray for strength to go through the fire so that God can purify you.

Day 2

What Is My Purpose?

Everyone wonders at one time or another, "Why am I here? Why was I born? What is my purpose?" Before you finish high school, the pressure will be on for you to choose a career path and to either enter that field or go to college in preparation for it. People who don't find the right job are usually miserable in their work. But there is a bigger purpose to our lives than finding a good job! Do you know what that purpose is? God does. He designed you specially to fulfill it.

Questions and Suggestions

- Read Philippians 2:12–15. According to this passage, what is God's purpose for us?
- Ask God to make you more aware of his purpose for you and to help you grow in that purpose.

Day 3
Pursuing Righteousness

We know that in his great love God pursues us. In fact, God has been called the "Hound of Heaven"—not a derogatory description but a compliment, emphasizing the way that God gets on our trail when we're lost and doesn't give up until he finds us (or we find him). God pursues us for a purpose—so that we can have eternal life with him, and abundant life now. But God also calls us to be "hounds"; we are to pursue righteousness, godliness, faith, love, endurance, and gentleness.

Questions and Suggestions

- Read 1 Timothy 6:11–16. What is the "all this" that we should flee from? What percentage of the time should we be doing these things?
- If there are any of these areas that you need to work on, ask God for his help. Submit your life to God's direction.

Day 4
Compassionate Clothing

Some people dress to make a statement; they want to shock others or to stand out in the crowd. Some people dress to be comfortable—sweats and a T-shirt, not caring what others think. Some people dress for utility—that is, their clothes fit their work: overalls for a farmer, suit and tie for a salesperson, a hairnet for a cook. God wants to clothe us in an outfit that makes a statement about his love; it's comfortable, and it helps us to do the work that God has called us to do.

Questions and Suggestions

- Read Colossians 3:12–17. How much compassion do you wear each day? How about kindness, gentleness, humility, and patience?
- Think of someone whom you can show compassion to today, and pray about doing that.

Day 5
Sheep and Goats

Jesus told some parables that are sometimes difficult to interpret. In one he seemed to praise a man's dishonesty; in another he seemed to compare God to a stubborn judge. Jesus often interpreted his parables at a later time for his disciples. But one time he talked about sheep and goats, and he explained things as he was saying them; there was no need for further clarification. The sheep and the goats represented two different groups into which Jesus will someday separate us—the sheep to inherit the Kingdom with him, the goats to be cast into eternal fire. Are you a sheep—or a goat?

Questions and Suggestions

- Read Matthew 25:31–46. Are you ready for the return of the Son of Man? Do you know people who need to know the Son of Man? Are you willing to share the Good News with them?
- Pray that when Jesus returns and you go to meet him, you can bring as many people as possible with you.

Leading a Teenager to Christ

Throughout the year, natural times may come up to share the plan of salvation with your students. When that opportunity arises, you will want to be ready with a simple explanation told in a noncoercive manner. You may want to write it out or go over in your mind ahead of time what you will say. Following is a suggested plan and some related scriptures to spark your own prayerful thinking.

Share these thoughts in your own words:

1. God loves you and offers a wonderful plan for your life (John 3:16 and John 10:10).
2. Each of us has sinned and been separated from God, preventing us from knowing and experiencing God's plan (Romans 3:23 and Romans 6:23).
3. Jesus Christ is God's provision for our sin and separation from God (Romans 5:8 and John 14:6).
4. When we place our faith in Jesus Christ as Savior and Lord, then we can know and experience God's love and plan for our lives (John 1:12 and Ephesians 2:8–9).

Receiving Christ involves turning to God from self (repentance) and trusting Christ to come into our lives to forgive our sins and to make us what God wants us to be. It is not enough to agree to a list of facts about Jesus Christ or to have an emotional experience. We receive Jesus Christ by *faith,* as an act of the *will.*

If a student indicates that he or she is ready to make a decision, ask that person if he or she has any questions. If all seems clear, encourage the student to pray a prayer of repentance, asking God's forgiveness. You might guide the student with the following prayer:

God, I know I've done wrong and gone my own way. I am sorry. I want to follow you. I know Jesus died for my sins. I accept Jesus as my Savior and Lord. Thank you for forgiving me. Thank you for the gift of eternal life.

After the student has prayed, thank God for hearing his or her prayer, and affirm the student as a new Christian.

Explain to your student that as we pray, read the Bible, worship with other Christians, and tell others about what God has done for us, God will help us know how to live. Christ's presence is with us to help us live God's way. One step that a new believer should take is to be baptized. Baptism tells others that we are serious about following Jesus. Jesus set the example in being baptized and we are baptized to show that we are living for Jesus.

Talk to your pastor and your student's parents about his or her decision. Continue to encourage your student by giving him or her instruction and materials for setting up a daily devotional time. If possible, make arrangements with someone in the church to meet regularly with your student to act as a spiritual mentor.

There are a number of simple tract-type visuals to help you share Christ with your students:

- It's Awesome! (available at www.warnerpress.org or 800-741-7721)
- Bridge to Life (available at www.navpress.com)
- The Answer (available at www.studentdiscipleship.org)

NOTES

EVALUATION FORM
The Call to Righteousness

Community size: _____   Church size: _____   Class size: _____

Average preparation time: _____   Class length:_____

My class is made up of:_____ Sixth graders   _____ Ninth graders

_____ Seventh graders   _____ Tenth graders

_____ Eighth graders   _____ Eleventh graders

_____ Twelfth graders

Please rate the following on a scale of 1 (never) to 10 (always):

- Were the instructions clear and user-friendly?   _____

- Was the content challenging enough for students?   _____

- Were the activities adequate for this age level?   _____

- Did you use the Portable Sanctuaries? (Y/N)   _____

- Did you use the Digital BRIDGES CD? (Y/N)   _____

Which sessions and areas worked best for you? _____

_____

Which sessions and areas should be changed or improved?_____

_____

Suggestions and Comments:_____

_____

_____

_____

Your full name:_____

Congregation Name, City, and State: _____

Phone number (_____)_____ E-mail _____

--fold here--

--fold here--

NAME_____

ADDRESS_____

CITY/STATE/ZIP_____

* Don't forget your return address! Postage is free!

‖‖‖

NO POSTAGE
NECESSARY
IF MAILED
IN THE
UNITED STATES

BUSINESS REPLY MAIL
FIRST-CLASS MAIL PERMIT NO. 1233 ANDERSON IN

POSTAGE WILL BE PAID BY ADDRESSEE

KEVIN STIFFLER, EDITOR
WARNER PRESS INC
PO BOX 2499
ANDERSON, IN 46018-2499

CPSIA information can be obtained
at www.ICGtesting.com
Printed in the USA
LVOW03s0917290316
481094LV00001B/2/P